WONDER WOMAN

THE ULTIMATE GUIDE TO THE AMAZON PRINCESS

20 X 3/08 (2/08)
23 X 7/11 (7/11)

LONDON, NEW YORK, MUNICH,
MELBOURNE, and DELHI

Senior Editor Alastair Dougall
Senior Designer Robert Perry
Designer Dan Bunyan
Publishing Manager Cynthia O'Neill
Publisher Alexandra Kirkham
Art Director Mark Richards
Production Nicola Torode
DTP Designer Eric Shapland

First American Edition, 2003

03 04 05 06 07 10 9 8 7 6 5 4 3 2 1

Published in the United States by DK Publishing, Inc.
375 Hudson Street, New York, New York 10014

Compilation copyright © 2003 Dorling Kindersley Limited

DK Publishing, Inc. offers special discounts for bulk purchases for sales promotions or premiums.
Specific, large-quantity needs can be met with special editions, including personalized covers, excerpts
of existing guides, and corporate imprints. For more information, contact Special Markets Department,
DK Publishing, Inc., 375 Hudson Street, New York, NY 10014 Fax: 800-600-9098.

Published in Great Britain by Dorling Kindersley Limited

Library of Congress Cataloging-in-Publication Data

Beatty, Scott, 1969-
  Wonder Woman : the ultimate guide to the Amazon princess / by Scott
Beatty.-- 1st American ed.
     p. cm.
Summary: Traces the sixty-year career of Wonder Woman with emphasis on
latest developments and characters and a timeline of key events.
Filmography: p.
Includes bibliographical references and index.
  ISBN 0-7894-9616-X (PLCJ)
  1. Wonder Woman (Comic strip)--juvenile literature. 2. Wonder Woman
(Fictitious character)--Juvenile literature. [1. Wonder Woman (Comic
strip) 2. Cartoons and comics.] I. Title.
  PN6728.W6B43 2003
  741.5'973--dc21
                                    2003011458

Color reproduction by Media Development and Printing Ltd., UK
Printed and bound in Italy by L.E.G.O.

Visit DC Comics online at www.dccomics.com or at keyword DC Comics on America Online.

Discover more at
www.dk.com

THE ULTIMATE GUIDE TO THE AMAZON PRINCESS

Written by
SCOTT BEATTY

Wonder Woman created by William Moulton Marston

CONTENTS

FOREWORD

HER NAME IS DIANA. Stronger than Heracles, wise as Athena, beautiful as Aphrodite, and swift as Hermes, she is the champion of the immortal Amazons of Themyscira, their Ambassador of Peace and Knowledge to the world of Man. She is Wonder Woman.

When William Moulton Marston created Wonder Woman in 1941, he imagined her as a hero who could save the world from the hatreds and wars of men. She was an Amazon princess named Diana who traveled to America, bringing to her new home "the eternal gifts of women: love and wisdom." Her mission was to lead the invincible youth of humanity against "the threatening forces of treachery, death, and destruction."

The character of Wonder Woman has been built around some powerful ideals. While Superman is an alpha male enforcer of American truth and justice, and Batman is a neurotic avenger who beats psychotic criminals into unconsciousness, Wonder Woman's mission in life is to teach human beings the ways of love, respect and peaceful coexistence.

By the time I was old enough to read, I was already a fan of Wonder Woman. Soon I began scouring books on classical mythology, looking for references to the ancient Greek legends that Marston had borrowed (and adapted) to create his feminist ideal. Wonder Woman has, literally, been a lifelong inspiration to me. She has given me drive and hope for a future where I was able to live out nearly every one of my dreams—including the opportunity to write and illustrate her comic-book adventures for over two years.

"Make a hawk a dove," the theme song shrieked from the *Wonder Woman* TV show. "Stop a war with love!" Some cynics believe that Diana's mission is doomed to failure; that human beings are destined for war and destruction. They think that Wonder Woman should toss aside her ideals and just pound the bad guys into submission instead of coaxing them with thoughtful, less violent options.

But they miss the point. Diana would never surrender to that kind of darkness. It's not in her nature. Heck, that's what makes her Wonder Woman! No matter what, she'll always strive to make the world a place of peace and love because she believes it's a better way than the alternative. And isn't it, really? I sure think so.

Phil Jimenez
New York City, April 2003

WONDER WOMAN'S WORLD

THE STORY OF WONDER WOMAN is an epic spanning over 30,000 years. It begins in prehistoric times, with the murder of a cavewoman heavy with child. The tale continues through the days of the ancient Greek culture and its pantheon of gods to our own, modern, war-torn world.

To Hippolyta, the childless Queen of the immortal Amazons, came the infant Diana, a gift from the gods of Mount Olympus. Hippolyta herself was a reincarnation of the very cavewoman who had suffered a cruel death all those millennia ago. And Diana, a daughter she molded from clay on the island of Themyscira, was that unborn child. Princess Diana was granted the wisdom of Athena, the beauty of Aphrodite, the speed of Hermes, and other miraculous powers by her patron gods and goddesses.

The day finally arrived when one of the Amazons would be chosen, following a grueling challenge of fighting skills, athletics, and wits, to become Themyscira's ambassador to Patriarch's World, the mortal realm of mankind. Though forbidden by Hippolyta to participate in the contest, Diana easily captured the much-prized mantle. Reluctantly, Hippolyta awarded her beloved daughter the talismans of her new office. Diana was armed with bulletproof bracelets that symbolized the Amazons' ancestral enslavement by Heracles. She also carried the Golden Lasso of Hestia, a lariat that compelled anyone bound in its finely forged links to speak only the truth.

Diana renounced her immortality and entered man's world to battle for peace and justice as the most legendary Amazon of all… WONDER WOMAN!

GODS OF OLYMPUS

THE DEITIES OF GREEK MYTH are among the mightiest beings in the whole of creation. They are the children of the Titans and the grandchildren of Gaea and Uranus, the earth and sky. Mostly, these gods are generous, but they only became so after Zeus, son of Cronus, deposed his Titan father from Mount Olympus and allowed his brothers and sisters and children to rule the heavens and the Earth and guide the destiny of mankind. The gods' dominion over humanity lasted for thousands of years. In time, however, their influence began to wane, and so they created the Amazons to lead mankind in the ways of virtue and keep the gods forever in people's hearts.

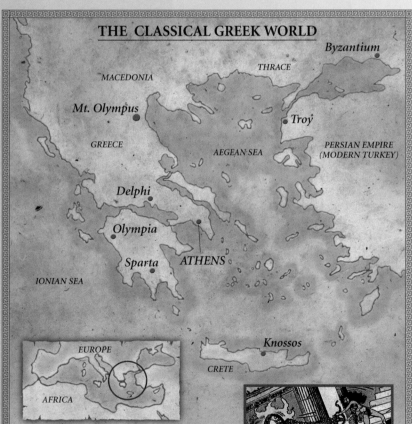

THE CLASSICAL GREEK WORLD

Byzantium
THRACE
MACEDONIA
Mt. Olympus
Troy
GREECE
AEGEAN SEA
PERSIAN EMPIRE
(MODERN TURKEY)
Delphi
Olympia
Sparta   ATHENS
IONIAN SEA

EUROPE
Knossos
CRETE
AFRICA

The gods of Olympus include (back row, l. to r.): Poseidon, Zeus, Hades; (middle row, l. to r.): Demeter, Hera, Apollo, Dionysus; (front row, l. to r.): Hermes, Aphrodite, Artemis, Athena, and Hestia.

Heracles, Zeus's son by a mortal woman, Alcmene.

THE FIRST OLYMPUS

Although there are far higher mountains on Earth, the mythical importance of Mount Olympus in northern Greece belies its humble elevation of 9,570 feet (2,917 meters). Since time immemorial, Mount Olympus was the home of the gods. Darkseid, an upstart "New God" from the distant world of Apokolips, destroyed the Olympian gods' halls and temples, but the legend of the first Olympus lives on.

Despite Wonder Woman's and Superman's best endeavors, Darkseid razed Mt. Olympus.

THE RULE OF MAN

For millennia, the Olympians have been content to preside over mankind. They sometimes enjoy meddling in human affairs, but in general they seek to guide humanity to greatness. Ares, Zeus's son and the God of War, has always argued that man should be conquered—and who better than him to do it!

A DIFFERENT WORLD
Mortal visitors to Mount Olympus would find the architecture unbelievably spectacular, but at the same time utterly anarchic and dizzying, with marble staircases ending in mid air and floors tilted at alarming angles. The normal earthly rules of gravity and the basic conventions of space and time mean absolutely nothing to the gods!

THE FATES
Even older than the Olympians, the three Fates—Clotho the spinner, Lachesis the tailor, and Atropos the shearer—are the mistresses of destiny. Their decrees—represented as a carefully measured thread marking an allotted span of time—must be followed both by god and man.

NEW OLYMPUS
Zeus joined with his elder brothers Hades and Poseidon to oust Cronus from Olympus. The brothers united once more to recreate the fabled home of the gods after Darkseid had obliterated it. No longer physically connected to its former mountain home in Greece, Mount Olympus now resides in a dimension adjacent to Earth. It is far enough removed for the gods' well-deserved privacy, but still close enough to permit the Olympians to watch over their beloved mortal believers.

QUEEN OF PARADISE

Hippolyta's crown as Queen of Themyscira.

The Girdle of Gaea, which magically protects the Amazons.

THE MURDER of a cavewoman more than 32,000 years ago, sowed the seeds of the Amazon race and its greatest champion. Hippolyta was that prehistoric female, pregnant with a child whose spirit would find its way back to her many millennia later. Reborn in the time of ancient Greece, Hippolyta and her Amazon sisters were created by the Gods of Mount Olympus to bring glory to Gaea, the Earth Mother. Dedicated to peace, the Amazons founded the city-state of Themyscira, ruled harmoniously by the queens Hippolyta and Antiope. However, a serpent lurked in paradise, and soon the fate of the Amazons would fall squarely upon Hippolyta's noble shoulders.

THE WELL OF SOULS

The life essences of Hippolyta and her unborn child were collected by Gaea and placed in the Well of Souls, which held all the spirits of women murdered throughout the ages. Five goddesses traveled to the Well to offer new life and purpose to the wailing souls longing to fulfil their destiny.

Antiope

Phthia

ANTIOPE AND PHTHIA

After the Amazons' escape from Heracles and Theseus, the tribe split into two factions, one peace-loving, led by Hippolyta, and one vengeful, commanded by her sister Antiope. Antiope was then murdered and Antiope's foster-daughter, Phthia, was falsely accused by a son of Theseus. Phthia led Antiope's Amazons to make war with mankind. They later settled in Egypt and founded the city of Bana-Mighdall.

THE AMAZONS EMERGE

As the goddesses Demeter, Aphrodite, Athena, Artemis, and Hestia watched, thousands of souls were called forth from Gaea's womb. The souls fell like rain into a lake and combined with the clay of the lake bed to form new human beings. Hippolyta rose first from the waves and was chosen as leader of this race of Amazon women alongside her sister Antiope. Both queens were given Girdles of Gaea, talismans that promised that none might resist the Amazons' power as long as neither girdle was removed. The Amazons then established the city-state of Themyscira in Asia Minor.

Demeter   *Aphrodite*   *Athena*   *Artemis*   *Hestia*

HERACLES

However, one Olympian did not support the creation of the Amazons. Ares, God of War, tolerated no one who stood in the way of his domination over mankind. Ares convinced Heracles, the son of Zeus, to lead his stepbrother Theseus and an army of men to make war on the Amazons. Queen Hippolyta wanted peace, but Heracles drugged the Amazon ruler, and stole the Girdle of Gaea from her. Without its protection, the Amazons were defenseless against him and his men!

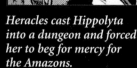

Heracles cast Hippolyta into a dungeon and forced her to beg for mercy for the Amazons.

AT WAR WITH MEN

Though shamed and beaten, Hippolyta did not lose hope. Her prayers were answered by Athena, who helped the Amazon queen to escape. The Amazons rallied and defeated Heracles and his brutal army. However the struggle only served to divide the Amazons into rival camps. While her sister Antiope continued on the path of war, Hippolyta urged her battle-weary sisters to renounce vengeance and depart Patriarch's World for the promise of paradise.

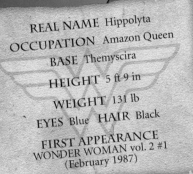

REAL NAME Hippolyta
OCCUPATION Amazon Queen
BASE Themyscira
HEIGHT 5 ft 9 in
WEIGHT 131 lb
EYES Blue   HAIR Black
FIRST APPEARANCE
WONDER WOMAN vol. 2 #1
(February 1987)

PARADISE FOUND

The Amazons' new home would also be called Themyscira. By the goddess Athena's decree, Hippolyta led her sisters to the shores of the Aegean Sea. The sea god Poseidon parted the waters for the Amazons to journey to an island paradise veiled from man. There, the Amazons were charged with guarding the evils of Pandora's Box, which were imprisoned deep under the ground. The Amazons became immortal and regained the purity of spirit robbed from them by Heracles.

THEMYSCIRA

THE GODDESSES of Mount Olympus had told the Amazons to lead mankind in the ways of peace. Yet, faced with men's hostility, the Amazons had angrily withdrawn from the world, and Heracles had enslaved them. Although the Olympians gave the Amazons the strength to deliver them from slavery, the gods decreed that Hippolyta and her sisters should journey to the land of Themyscira. There, on this secret island barred from mortal man, the Amazons would live as immortals and reclaim their purity of spirit as they guarded over Doom's Doorway and the unspeakable evils that lay beneath it.

AMAZON ASYLUM

Poseidon, god of the seas, parted the waters of the Atlantic Ocean for the Amazons to begin their long journey to Themyscira. But upon their arrival, Hippolyta and her sisters were rejuvenated with immortality. They began to clear the forest and ready Themyscira for habitation. The chief architect Timandra designed a great city honoring the sisters' heroic history and glorifying their mighty Olympian benefactors with temples erected to their devotion.

PARADISE ISLAND

The Amazons lived serenely on Themyscira for more than 3,000 years, concealed from "Patriarch's World"—the domain of mortal man—by the gods' wiles. They never knew the pains of aging or hunger, and they wore their bracelets, a symbol of their former bondage, as a reminder to never again forsake their patron gods and goddesses. The Amazons remained warriors, but achieved a perfect harmony between body and spirit.

PARADISE LOST!

The Imperiex War threatened not just Earth, but creation itself. The Amazons of Themyscira joined an alliance of alien worlds in defense of Earth, the focal point of Imperiex's campaign and the target of an energy-tendril that would trigger a new Big Bang. To prevent universal oblivion, the Amazons sacrificed Themyscira, using a mystical enchantment to transport the island into outer space. There it served as Earth's last line of defense. Unfortunately, Paradise Island was lost to the tendril's advance, but its destruction gave Diana and her sisters time to regroup and mount a successful attack upon Imperiex's forces.

The city of the Bana-Mighdall was the last remnant of Themyscira to fall before Imperiex's all-consuming energy tendril pulverized Paradise Island!

1) ROYAL PALACE
The center of the Amazon matriarchy, the Royal Palace at the heart of the Capitol Mall was constructed from the finest marble.

2) SENATE CHAMBER
Though Queen Hippolyta was the final arbiter of Themysciran law, the Senate allowed every Amazon a voice in the governing of the immortal sisterhood amid the hallowed Halls of Justice.

3) THRONE ROOM
The seat of Queen Hippolyta's power and the place where the lonely, reincarnated ruler often wished for the child she seemed forever denied.

4) BANA-MIGHDALL
The far side of Themyscira, once a barren wasteland, was made habitable by the Egyptian Amazons who established their own city there.

HIDDEN ISLAND
Athena, goddess of wisdom, cloaked Themyscira in a bank of protective clouds. The island was situated within what would become known as the "Bermuda Triangle." This region became renowned for a number of mysterious disappearances of ships and aircraft.

The Coliseum

City of the Dead

5) THE MYSTICAL AREAS
The enchanted forest was given new life by Queen Hippolyta's touch. The whirlpool Charybdis, the Harpies' Aerie, and the Lair of Medusa existed in these magical arbors.

6) DOOM'S DOORWAY
The entrance to Pandora's Box was well guarded to ensure that the evils chained below never escaped again to bring chaos to Earth.

7) THE GROVE
Marked by a statue memorializing Hippolyta's sister Antiope, Diana's favorite arbor was a veritable Garden of Eden.

8) THE NECROPOLIS
Beneath a dark temple of the same name rested the infamous City of the Dead, where the Amazons killed in battle reside for eternity.

9) ISLE OF HEALING
Also known as "Transformation Island," the Amazon's medicinal arts were practiced here to heal the sick of body or mind.

10) DIANA TREVOR
A monument to Princess Diana's namesake, who fought alongside the Amazons at Doom's Doorway, stood within the Hall of Heroes, which honored those women who had given their lives in defense of Themyscira.

THE AMAZONS

UPON THEIR MIRACULOUS BIRTHS the Amazons were graced with bountiful gifts by the goddesses of Olympus. Athena gave them wisdom to help them follow the paths of truth and justice; Artemis granted them hunting skills; Demeter promised them plentiful harvests; Hestia helped them build the city of Themyscira; Aphrodite gave them the gift of love; and Gaea made the Amazons strong and powerful. After escaping slavery by warmongering men hostile to their ideals, the Amazons withdrew from the world to embrace peace on an island paradise where men were forbidden.

BLESSED BY GODS

The Amazons tried to lead humanity in the ways of virtue so that all men could know the Olympians and worship them always. Thousands of years after their creation, the Amazons still celebrate their origins in the annual "Feast of Five" honoring the goddesses who gave them another chance at life.

THE CODE OF THE AMAZONS

LET ALL WHO READ THESE WORDS KNOW: WE ARE A NATION OF WOMEN, DEDICATED TO OUR SISTERS, TO OUR GODS, AND TO THE PEACE THAT IS HUMANKIND'S RIGHT. GRANTED LIFE BY GAEA, THE GODDESSES, AND THE SOULS OF WOMEN PAST, WE HAVE BEEN GIFTED WITH THE MISSION TO UNITE THE PEOPLE OF OUR WORLD WITH LOVE AND COMPASSION.

MAN HAS CORRUPTED MANY OF THE LAWS OUR GODS SET FORTH. SO, IN THEIR WISDOM, THE GODDESSES DID CREATE A RACE OF FEMALE WARRIORS DEDICATED TO THE IDEALS OF UNITING ALL PEOPLE, ALL SEXES, ALL RACES, ALL CREEDS. NO LONGER WILL MAN RULE ALONE, FOR NOW WOMAN STANDS AS AN EQUAL TO TEMPER HIS AGGRESSION WITH COMPASSION, LEND REASON TO HIS RAGES, AND OVERCOME HATRED WITH LOVE.

WE ARE THE AMAZONS, AND WE HAVE COME TO SAVE MANKIND.

VICTORY OVER MEN

Although not created for war, the Amazons had the strength to prevail when Heracles and his armies overran Themyscira. Following their victory, the Amazons loyal to Queen Hippolyta left behind the death and destruction of man's world. Others, led by Queen Antiope, renounced the Olympians and embraced war as the path to their survival. For centuries, the two tribes lived apart until another conflict reconciled them.

THE AMAZON WAY

Despite being cut off from ordinary mortals on Themyscira, the Amazons fulfilled the peace-loving dreams of the goddesses of Olympus by guarding the world from the nightmares of Pandora's Box. These creatures were all imprisoned behind Doom's Doorway. Without the eternal vigilance of the Amazons, the world would have been destroyed many times over. The Amazons also pursued knowledge and the arts. Little by little, by staying true to the principles of the goddesses who had created them, they found peace and happiness.

NOTABLE AMAZONS

Artists and artisans, soldiers and scholars, the Amazons are a highly gifted people. Over the past 3,000 years, these are just some who have distinguished themselves:

1) Cydippe: an aid to the Amazon Princess. **2)** Myrhha: once Hippolyta's chambermaid, she fought and died bravely saving Earth from Imperiex. **3)** Pallas: the ingenious smith who created Diana's golden eagle armor. **4)** Mala: a close friend of Diana's who competed in the second contest to choose a Wonder Woman. **5)** Clio: a royal scribe. **6)** Mnemosyne: an historian. **7)** Aella: renowned falconer who died during the Amazon civil wars. **8)** Niobe: a priestess. **9)** Oenone: chief botanist. **10)** Epione: chief healer. **11)** Phthia: Queen Antiope's adopted daughter and the spiritual teacher of Julia Kapetelis. **12)** Timandra: chief architect of Themyscira. **13)** Penelope: priestess and lover of Menalippe. **14)** Euboea: a captain in the Amazon royal guard. **15)** Menalippe: former priestess who died during the War of the Gods. **16)** Phillipus: General of the Amazon guard and Queen Hippolyta's most trusted advisor; currently Chancellor of Themyscira. **17)** Hellene: sculptor; killed by the Cheetah.

SACRED CEREMONY

Though granted eternal youth by the gods, Amazons can die like any mortal. When the tyrant Darkseid attacked the Amazons' ranks in a bloody war between his planet Apokolips and Themyscira, more than 1,200 Amazons lost their lives. Their bodies lay upon funeral biers awaiting the sacred ceremony of purifying flame that would carry the souls of the fallen to the afterlife's everlasting rest.

TURNED TO STONE

The Amazons once faced the prospect of being stone statues forever when the Olympic gods left Earth and unknowingly took with them the powers that gave the Amazons life. Separated from their patron deities, the Amazons reverted to the clay from which they had been formed. Only when the gods eventually returned to Earth were the Amazons able to become living and breathing beings once more.

THE LOST TRIBE

WHEN HIPPOLYTA'S sister queen Antiope was killed by Ariadne, Theseus's jealous former wife, Antiope's adopted daughter Phthia led Antiope's Amazons into the Egyptian desert. There this "Lost Tribe" founded the city-state of Bana-Mighdall. Unlike Hippolyta's Amazons, the Bana-Mighdall sisterhood had forsaken eternal life by rejecting the Olympian Gods in favor of other pantheons. To replenish their numbers, this warlike tribe of mercenary assassins made slave husbands out of men they captured.

LOST GODDESSES
The patron deities of the Bana-Mighdall include (l. to r.) the goddesses Mammitu, Isis, and Neith.

AT WAR WITH MANKIND
Antiope's Amazons chose the path to war while those loyal to Hippolyta found peace in paradise. Antiope's "Lost Tribe" renounced the Girdle of Gaea in the belief that they were forging their own destiny. In truth, the evil sorceress Circe had duped them.

SHIM'TAR

The Bana-Mighdall selects its chief warrior in a rite of combat known as the Tournament of the Crown. The victor is called "Shim'Tar," and receives a high-tech Bana-Mighdall battlesuit. Wonder Woman met the first Shim'Tar—her identity unrevealed—during her quest to recover her magic lasso. Later, Circe transformed Hippolyta into Shim'Tar and pitted her against Diana. A young Bana-Mighdall named Akila became Shim'Tar not long after and augmented the battlesuit with science and sorcery before injuries during the Amazon Civil War forced her to cede the role to Artemis.

Artemis now holds the mantle of Shim'Tar and pledges to protect all Amazons, be they Themysciran or Bana-Mighdall.

Circe transported hundreds of Bana-Mighdall warriors to Themyscira to foment war. One of them, Artemis—just 14 years old—stood against the invasion of paradise.

AMAZONS ATTACK!

Ironically, Wonder Woman's feline foe the Cheetah helped reunite the Amazons with their Bana-Mighdall sisters. Barbara Minerva stole Diana's golden lasso—forged from the Girdle of Gaea originally belonging to Antiope—and used it to divine the location of Hippolyta's Girdle. With Wonder Woman on her trail, Minerva discovered the "Lost Tribe" and their hidden city. The Bana-Mighdall helped Diana capture the Cheetah; however the Egyptian army then destroyed the hidden city.

Kadesha Banu was High Priestess, Master Methodologist, and Supreme Alchemist of the Bana-Mighdall. The venom in her cobra dart helped the Lost Tribe subdue Wonder Woman.

Anahid was queen of the Bana-Mighdall. She allied herself with Wonder Woman and was later slain by the Cheetah.

Nehebka became queen after Anahid's death. She was murdered after revealing the Lost Tribe's history to Diana.

CIVIL WARS

After the Egyptian army's onslaught, the Lost Tribe's city was swallowed up by the desert sands; however many of the Bana-Mighdall survived and were sheltered by Circe. When Hippolyta journeyed to the United Nations as a show of goodwill, Circe loosed Bana-Mighdall warriors upon the proceedings to blacken the Amazons' name. Circe later transported the Lost Tribe to Themyscira and sparked the first of two Amazon civil wars.

>ULP<

POSSESSED BY EVIL

Few among the Amazons paid much attention to the deformed Themysciran witch Magala. And not one Amazon noticed when Magala died casting one of her spells. However, Circe did and used the opportunity to plant the soul of vengeful Ariadne within Magala's body. And with both Amazons and Bana-Mighdall oblivious to her scheming, Magala engineered new civil unrest between the two tribes.

THE SISTERHOOD UNITED

Many died during the second Amazon Civil War. The conflict ended when Fury—enraged that her beloved Hippolyta was threatened—tore Magala's heart from her chest. Thereafter, Hippolyta abolished the Themysciran monarchy and set the stage for democracy to govern both tribes. Although united as equals, neither side embraced one another as true sisters until the Imperiex War. At last they stood together to face a common foe and to avenge Hippolyta, who had given her life in defense of the Amazon sisterhood upon the shattered remnants of Themyscira.

FOR THE AMAZONS!

FOR THEMYSCIRA! FOR HIPPOLYTA!

When Hippolyta perished, Artemis of the Bana-Mighdall and General Phillipus of the Amazons joined forces to rebuild paradise in her honor.

THE BIRTH OF DIANA

IMMORTALITY CAN BE a lonely existence. Hippolyta and her Amazon sisters enjoyed peace and prosperity on Themyscira for 3,000 years, but the reincarnated Queen longed for the child she had been denied in her previous life. The oracle Menalippe told her to mold a baby out of clay. Hippolyta did so and waited for a miracle. The goddesses of Olympus granted life to the child—a girl Hippolyta named Diana—giving her the soul of the unborn infant lost to Hippolyta some 32,000 years before! And so Diana became the first child ever born on Themyscira.

A WONDERFUL CHILD

With powers granted by the goddesses of Olympus, Diana quickly grew strong. And with a thousand aunts and sisters to guide her, she swiftly mastered the ways of the Amazons. Her appetite for learning was voracious and Diana soon mastered all the skills of a warrior. She became expert at archery, swordplay, and all the martial arts practiced on Themyscira for thousands of years.

BURDEN OF POWERS

Diana's great strength, a gift from the goddess Demeter, was sometimes too much for her to control. Diana could lift a mighty oak as if it were nothing, but this same strength could crush a flower to paste. Thus, with Hippolyta's blessing, the Amazon General Phillipus began to train Diana to help her make full use of her powers by first controlling them.

A TERRIBLE LESSON

One night a throng of cloaked warriors ambushed Diana. Believing it to be one of Phillipus's tests, Diana gave her attackers a brutal beating. But when she saw the faces of her victims, friends and sister Amazons all, she felt great remorse and vowed to be mindful of her strength and the damage it could inflict.

GENERAL PHILLIPUS

General Phillipus, the
Amazons' greatest warrior,
was Hippolyta's most trusted advisor. Thanks to Phillipus's guidance, Diana learned to control her strength, speed, and power of flight, her wisdom and her wits. However, Diana came to rely on her abilities too much, forgetting to protect herself. She learned another painful lesson when Phillipus shot the prideful princess with an arrow to teach her that too much faith in her powers could leave her vulnerable.

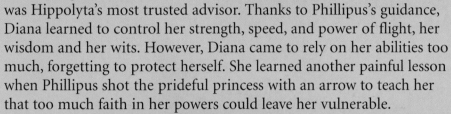

DIANA TREVOR

As a teenager, Diana Rockwell loved to fly. She later married U. S. Air Force Lt. Ulysses S. Trevor—their son Steve would inherit his parents' love of flying. But family life did not satisfy Diana Trevor. She served as a pilot in the Women's Auxiliary Ferrying Squadron in World War II, and then became a test pilot. In 1948, Diana flew a prototype Sabre jet plane into the Bermuda Triangle, piercing the clouds concealing Themyscira. A lightning bolt destroyed her plane and she parachuted into the stormy sea, swimming past the whirlpool Charybdis to reach the island. She found the Amazons battling the many-handed monster Cottus at Doom's Doorway. Her .45 automatic blazing, Diana killed Cottus, but lost her life. As Diana lay dying, she whispered her name to Hippolyta, who named her own child Diana in Diana Trevor's honor.

THANKING THE GODS

Diana made sure her Olympian benefactors knew how grateful she was for her powers. Every day she gave thanks to Demeter, Aphrodite, Athena, Artemis, Hestia, and Hermes. She promised not to waste her abilities and swore an oath to protect the innocent and always seek the path to peace.

As Wonder Woman, Diana wears the standard of her namesake, Diana Rockwell Trevor. Her warrior's garb confirms her as the most honored Amazon of Themyscira.

THE CONTEST

Angry at what he saw as humanity's disrespect for the gods, the war god Ares announced that he would inflict war on humanity. Zeus, king of the gods, decreed that the Amazons should hold a contest to choose an ambassador to man's world to counteract the threat of Ares. Diana decided to enter the contest, but in secret. She proved herself the keenest of eye and the fleetest of foot, as well as the mightiest of warriors. As the last woman standing, Diana's reward was a pair of unbreakable silver bracelets and the mantle of Wonder Woman!

THE FINAL TEST

Diana had a final test to face. General Phillipus fired Diana Trevor's .45 at her. With breathtaking speed, Diana deflected each bullet with her bracelets. Hippolyta reluctantly accepted that her daughter was the Amazon's champion.

WONDER WOMAN'S STYLE

"OLD GLORY" and the mantle of Wonder Woman have much in common. The Amazon coat-of-arms was inspired by American aviatrix Diana Rockwell Trevor. During World War II, Trevor crash-landed on Themyscira while serving in the U. S. Women's Auxiliary Ferrying Squadron. She later died defending the Themyscirans against creatures loosed from Doom's Doorway. The badges and pins on Trevor's flight jacket and the American flag she wore became the major design motifs for the costume of Wonder Woman!

STAR-SPANGLED BANNER

Queen Hippolyta named her child Diana for Diana Trevor, who saved the Amazons from certain destruction. Upon winning a contest to represent Themyscira in Patriarch's World, young Diana went one step further and donned garb inspired by the red, white, and blue standard of freedom and democracy Trevor wore on her sleeve.

Diana's tiara is razor-sharp and can be hurled like a boomerang.

Diana's emblem is recognized the world over.

Bracelets can deflect bullets.

Hestia's Lasso of Truth.

REAL NAME Diana
OCCUPATION Ambassador of Peace
BASE Themysciran Embassy, New York City
HEIGHT 5 ft 11 in
WEIGHT 140 lb
EYES Blue HAIR Black
FIRST APPEARANCE
ALL STAR COMICS #8 (Winter 1941)

BLACK SUIT

Diana was once deemed unworthy of her office as messenger of peace. The Themysciran High Council called for a new contest to choose its ambassador to Patriarch's World. This time, Artemis raced to victory. Artemis briefly possessed the Lasso of Truth, but Diana continued to operate as an "unofficial" Wonder Woman, wearing a star-spangled black costume in honor of Diana Trevor.

In royal regalia, Diana addresses the United Nations.

ROBES OF CRIMSON

As the Amazon ambassador to Patriarch's World, Diana dons crimson robes when attending state functions. These robes once marked Diana's royal status as Princess of Themyscira. However, following the death of her mother, Queen Hippolyta, Diana forsook her crown. Themyscira is now a democracy under Phillipus, Chancellor of the Amazon archipelago.

GLADIATRIX

As messenger of peace, Diana knows that war is the course of last resort. However, during the "War of the Gods," she took up Amazonian armor and weapons, to defeat the minions of Circe.

Collapsed "bubble-less" Neoprene and Lycra weave.

DIVING SUIT

Amazons are natural swimmers, often performing high dives off sheer cliffs into the deep Atlantic waters below Themyscira. Diana's wardrobe includes a modified diving suit for oceanic adventures. This version features triple-interlock stitching and minimal seams to insulate Diana from freezing-cold temperatures at great depths.

BATTLE ARMOR

Wonder Woman's battle armor is modeled upon the eagle, a symbol of strength and freedom. The stars and stripes of the American flag decorate Diana's armor in honor of her namesake, Diana Trevor.

IMMORTAL IMAGE

Diana's "death" at the hands of the demon Neron briefly led to her rebirth as a goddess! Dressed accordingly, she joined the pantheon of Olympus as the Goddess of Truth.

WONDER-MAKEOVER!

When Wonder Woman found herself suffering from amnesia and set upon by mysterious assailants, she sought shelter with Becca Doherty, perhaps the Amazing Amazon's greatest fan. Becca helped Diana hide by trimming her long raven tresses. With a pair of eyeglasses added to her short new hairstyle, Diana barely recognized herself!

WONDER POWERS

FIVE GODDESSES AND ONE GOD gave Diana the powers she possesses as Wonder Woman. Aphrodite gave her beauty and a loving heart. Athena granted her wisdom. Hestia gave Diana the power to open men's hearts to help them heed her message of peace. The other immortals imbued Diana with awe-inspiring abilities that would set her apart from her Amazon sisters.

THE STRENGTH OF GAEA

When Queen Hippolyta molded a baby from the clay of Themyscira, the goddess Gaea—the Earth-mother herself—gave the child life, and the goddess Demeter granted Hippolyta's daughter, Diana, amazing strength. Wonder Woman can hoist broken bridges back into place and lift whole trains while barely breaking sweat. In fact, Wonder Woman could even be as strong as the Man of Steel himself—Superman!

THE POWER TO FLY

Hermes, Messenger of the Gods, was the only male Olympian to endow Diana with miraculous abilities. His gifts was the powers of flight and of speed. Wonder Woman can fly faster than sound travels, but she cannot soar too high. As a mortal, she still requires protection against the vacuum of space. On the ground, however, Diana is so fast she can deflect bullets with her silver bracelets.

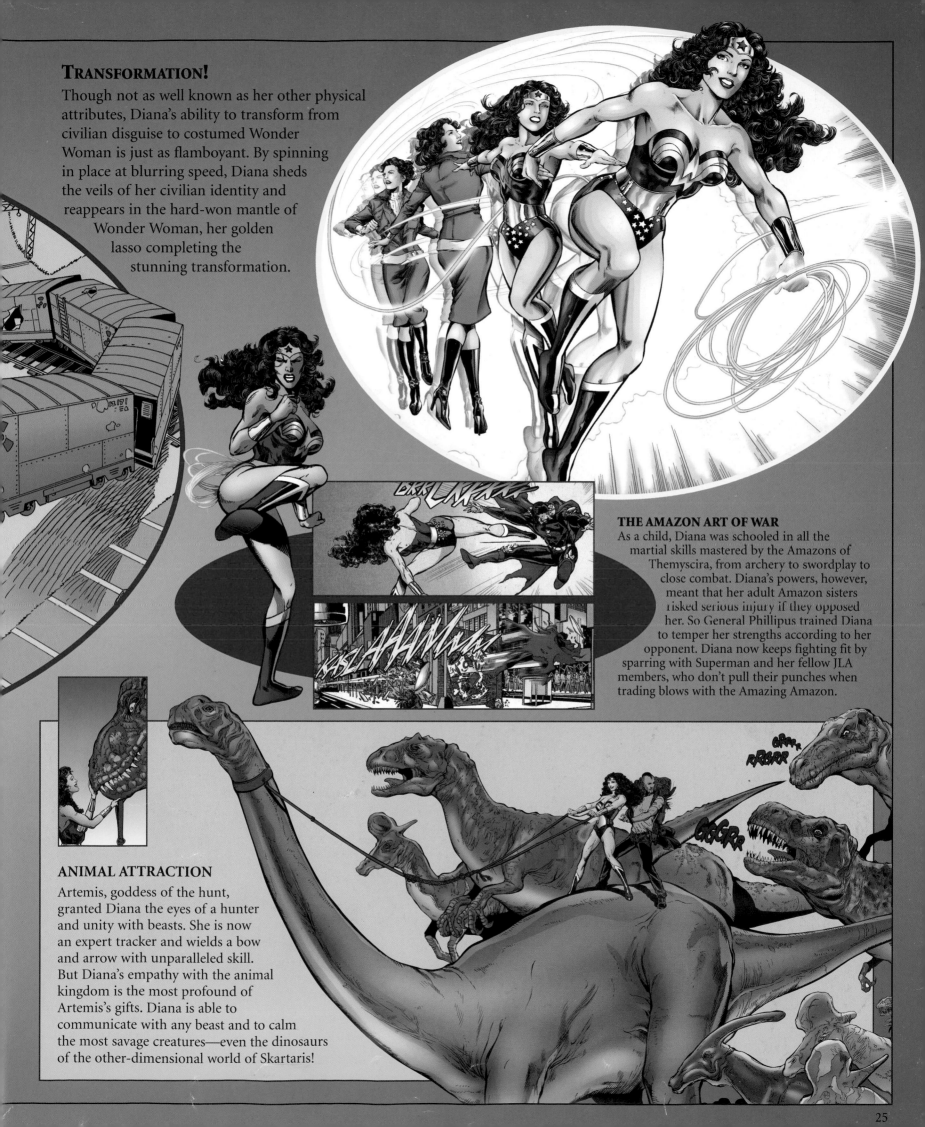

TRANSFORMATION!

Though not as well known as her other physical attributes, Diana's ability to transform from civilian disguise to costumed Wonder Woman is just as flamboyant. By spinning in place at blurring speed, Diana sheds the veils of her civilian identity and reappears in the hard-won mantle of Wonder Woman, her golden lasso completing the stunning transformation.

THE AMAZON ART OF WAR

As a child, Diana was schooled in all the martial skills mastered by the Amazons of Themyscira, from archery to swordplay to close combat. Diana's powers, however, meant that her adult Amazon sisters risked serious injury if they opposed her. So General Phillipus trained Diana to temper her strengths according to her opponent. Diana now keeps fighting fit by sparring with Superman and her fellow JLA members, who don't pull their punches when trading blows with the Amazing Amazon.

ANIMAL ATTRACTION

Artemis, goddess of the hunt, granted Diana the eyes of a hunter and unity with beasts. She is now an expert tracker and wields a bow and arrow with unparalleled skill. But Diana's empathy with the animal kingdom is the most profound of Artemis's gifts. Diana is able to communicate with any beast and to calm the most savage creatures—even the dinosaurs of the other-dimensional world of Skartaris!

WEAPONS OF PEACE

EVEN A WARRIOR FOR PEACE must sometimes wield more than words in the struggle to end aggression. Among Wonder Woman's cache of personal weapons are gifts from the Greek gods themselves, notably her bullet-deflecting silver bracelets and unbreakable golden lasso, talismans that are literal reminders of her Amazon oath to uphold freedom and defend truth for all mankind. Her ruby-inlaid tiara, once a crown of royalty, is a symbol of Wonder Woman's status as the world's greatest super heroine. Other armaments reflect the martial disciplines of her native Themyscira, the "Paradise Island" where Diana first learned to fight for the cause of love.

LASSO OF TRUTH
Diana's Lasso of Truth was bequeathed to her by the goddess Hestia. Forged by Hephaestus from the golden Girdle of Gaea, the Lasso was carried down from Mount Olympus slung to the shaft of an arrow shot by Artemis herself.

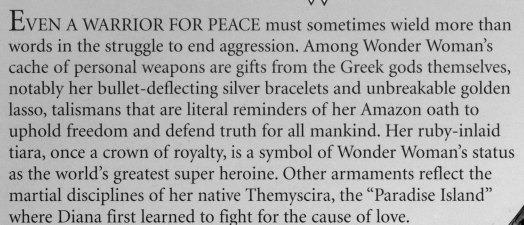

YOU'RE BOUND IN THE *LASSO* OF HESTIA. YOU'LL NEVER BREAK ITS BONDS.

SO STOP TRYING AND *LISTEN* TO ME.

IN THE LOOP
A lariat of tiny chain links, the Lasso of Truth is of limitless length and virtually indestructible. Neither god nor mortal can escape the Lasso, which compels anyone bound by it to speak the absolute truth.

AMAZON BRACELETS

An Amazon's bracelets represent her warrior sisterhood's ancient enslavement by Heracles. The bracelets remind the Amazons of a subjugation that they will never again endure. Diana's silver bracelets are unique, forged by Hephaestus from the shards of Zeus's Aegis (shield) as a prize for the most worthy Amazon. Diana won the bulletproof bracelets in the contest to represent Themyscira in Patriarch's World as Wonder Woman.

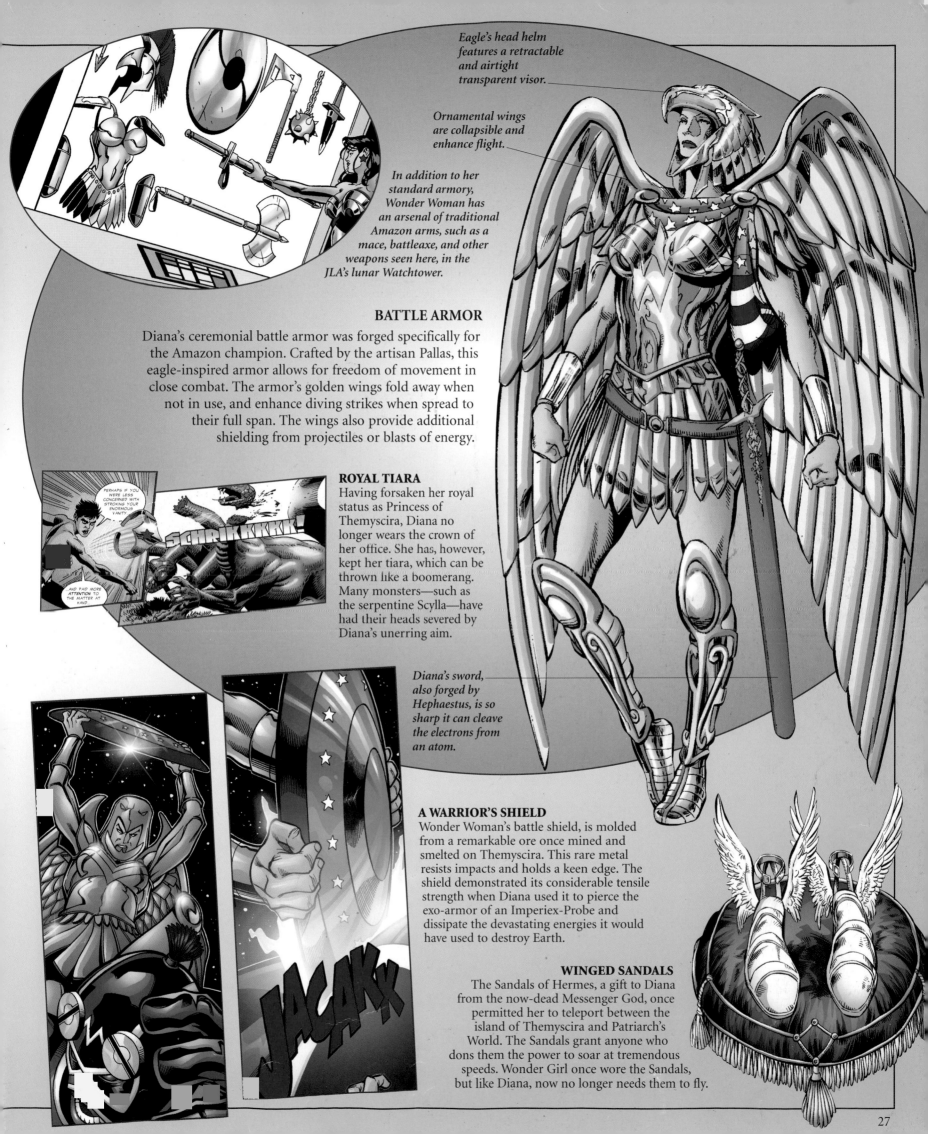

Eagle's head helm features a retractable and airtight transparent visor.

Ornamental wings are collapsible and enhance flight.

In addition to her standard armory, Wonder Woman has an arsenal of traditional Amazon arms, such as a mace, battleaxe, and other weapons seen here, in the JLA's lunar Watchtower.

BATTLE ARMOR

Diana's ceremonial battle armor was forged specifically for the Amazon champion. Crafted by the artisan Pallas, this eagle-inspired armor allows for freedom of movement in close combat. The armor's golden wings fold away when not in use, and enhance diving strikes when spread to their full span. The wings also provide additional shielding from projectiles or blasts of energy.

ROYAL TIARA

Having forsaken her royal status as Princess of Themyscira, Diana no longer wears the crown of her office. She has, however, kept her tiara, which can be thrown like a boomerang. Many monsters—such as the serpentine Scylla—have had their heads severed by Diana's unerring aim.

PERHAPS IF YOU WERE LESS CONCERNED WITH STROKING YOUR ENORMOUS VANITY

SCHRIKKKKK!

...AND PAID MORE ATTENTION TO THE MATTER AT HAND...

Diana's sword, also forged by Hephaestus, is so sharp it can cleave the electrons from an atom.

A WARRIOR'S SHIELD

Wonder Woman's battle shield, is molded from a remarkable ore once mined and smelted on Themyscira. This rare metal resists impacts and holds a keen edge. The shield demonstrated its considerable tensile strength when Diana used it to pierce the exo-armor of an Imperiex-Probe and dissipate the devastating energies it would have used to destroy Earth.

JAGAKK

WINGED SANDALS

The Sandals of Hermes, a gift to Diana from the now-dead Messenger God, once permitted her to teleport between the island of Themyscira and Patriarch's World. The Sandals grant anyone who dons them the power to soar at tremendous speeds. Wonder Girl once wore the Sandals, but like Diana, now no longer needs them to fly.

MIRACLE VEHICLES

WONDER WOMAN seems to have vehicles of every type at her disposal—the only element they have in common is that they are *invisible*. However, even more astounding is that all of these wonderful wheeled, flying, or submerging vehicles are different aspects of the *same* miraculous machine! This super-advanced technology came from an alien world and is capable of transforming into any vehicle Wonder Woman wishes for, whether she chooses to travel in an invisible jet, a deep-sea submersible or a horse-drawn battle chariot.

SIGHTLESS SUPER-RACE
The Lansinarians' scientific advances inadvertently brought about their downfall.

A graviton web shields passengers from the G-forces of sudden acceleration or deceleration.

THE LANSANARIANS

40,000 years ago, mankind's oldest ancestors retreated beneath the then-lush continent of Antarctica when their own science inadvertently started an ice age. The Lansanarians burrowed deep underground, where darkness and evolution made them sightless. Four of them remained on Earth's surface and transformed into the beast-headed gods who inspired ancient Egypt to greatness.

HIGH-TECH CHARIOT

Soon after gaining the Lansinar technology, Diana learned that it was part of an extraterrestrial artifact called The Ring. This technology even briefly adapted itself to become the WonderDome, Diana's floating base above Gateway City. Winged chariots could be detached from the Dome's superstructure to convey visitors back and forth to the Themysciran-inspired structure.

THE GREAT GIFT
Aided by Heracles in his guise as Champion, as well as Cave Carson and his team of spelunkers, Wonder Woman saved Lansinar and Earth from disaster! In their gratitude, the Lansanarians gave Diana the amazing artifact that would become her Invisible Jet. This alien technology had shaped itself to the needs of the Lansinarians, providing them with the perfect exploratory craft. While the Lansanarians explained its properties to Wonder Woman, the substance morphed from submarine to spacecraft!

GRAVITON TECHNOLOGY

The Invisible Jet harnesses graviton particles—electrically-neutral, gravity-defying quantum particles—for subsonic propulsion through air and space. If stranded in orbit, the Jet can reprocess Diana's breath for up to two hours of breathable oxygen.

For offensive purposes, the Invisible jet is capable of fashioning projectile weapons out of its own substance, although doing so depletes the mass of its fuselage.

DON'T BE AFRAID AS IT *UNSHAPES* ITSELF TO RELEASE US.

IT'S COMPOSED OF A SPECIAL TECHNOLOGY; IT CAN TAKE WHATEVER *FORM* I NEED IT TO.

MORPHING MATERIAL

Hippolyta took the Lansinarian vehicle with her when she traveled back to war-torn 1942. The technology adapted its appearance to suit the era, morphing into a prop-driven plane. Diana knew the technology was in good hands when, disguised as Miss America, she helped Hippolyta battle Nazis!

AIRCRAFT OF THE FUTURE

The latest version of Wonder Woman's Invisible Jet, perhaps the most advanced aircraft ever conceived, was designed by Amazon engineers. When the Amazons took up the challenge of rebuilding shattered Themyscira, Diana asked the WonderDome to contribute its techno-biological secrets to the reconstruction effort. New Themyscira now features Amazon architecture that possesses miraculous adaptive qualities. However Lansinarian technology is still present in the Invisible Jet, which remains one of the most versatile and important elements in Wonder Woman's arsenal.

Wonder Woman has her own hangar on the Themysciran islands for the Invisible Jet.

WONDER-CYCLE!

Self-regenerating and thought-controlled, the Invisible Jet can morph in the blink of an eye into any other vehicle Wonder Woman desires. When Diana traveled to North Carolina to visit close friend Trevor Barnes and his nephew Bobby (one of Wonder Woman's biggest fans), she rode into town in style on a flying Invisible Motorcycle!

It may mimic a gasoline-fueled motorcycle, but graviton-propelled Lansinarian technology is pollution-free and much faster!

29

DEATH AND REBIRTH

THE GODS GAVE DIANA LIFE, but in the blink of an eye a devil stole that spark from her. Wonder Woman first met the demon Neron when he gave scores of supervillains augmented powers in exchange for their souls (bargains that many would bitterly regret for all eternity). To prevent hell on Earth, Diana joined her fellow heroes and heroines and defeated Neron's army of demonic adversaries. She also saved Captain Marvel from this devil's dark influence. For these acts of courage, the Amazing Amazon and her peace-loving peers would one day face the full fury of this underworld lord's hatred!

ETRIGAN THE DEMON

Back in the days of King Arthur's court at Camelot, the magician Merlin conjured the Demon Etrigan to battle the forces of evil sorceress Morgaine Le Fay. Although King Arthur and his knights perished, Merlin survived and bound Etrigan's demonic power to a peasant, so that the Demon might continue to fight evil. Jason Blood has lived for more than a thousand years as the vessel for a thing of unspeakable power and ferocity.

DEATH BLAST

To have his revenge, Neron transported Wonder Woman and several of her allies, as well as Etrigan the Demon, to his hellish underworld. He separated Etrigan from his human host, Jason Blood, then blasted the life from Wonder Woman!

A FALLEN AMAZON

How could Neron slay the Amazing Amazon, who had been given great powers by the Gods? Only Neron knew that Diana's powers were divided between herself and Artemis, a result of the spell that the sorceress Magala had cast upon Diana during the second contest. Thus weakened, Diana was easy prey for Neron. With a blast of sickly, greenish hellfire, Wonder Woman was no more!

With Diana fading fast, desperate measures were needed. The Martian Manhunter morphed himself into an exact duplicate of Diana's central nervous system and slipped into her body, aligning himself precisely to her every cell. He became a conduit for a massive jolt of electromagnetic power from Superman that the heroes hoped would jumpstart her life forces!

CLINGING TO LIFE

As Diana fell, reinforcements arrived in the underworld. Neron skulked away while the Amazons returned to Earth with Diana's near-lifeless body. Diana's friends and family held a silent vigil by her bedside—then help arrived in a flash of blue lightning. First came Superman—briefly blessed with energy powers—and soon followed by the entire Justice League of America!

GREAT HERA!

However, not even Superman and the Martian Manhunter could save Diana. She finally died when the diabolical Dr. Doris Zeul attempted to steal her comatose body and transfer her own consciousness into it! While the JLA and the rest of Diana's extended family were numb with grief, Hippolyta refused to lose faith in miracles. The woman who had once prayed to her gods to breathe life into a clay doll beseeched the goddess Hera to restore Diana. And with a flash of golden fire, Wonder Woman was reborn!

Morgue workers at Gateway Memorial Hospital looked on in stunned disbelief as Wonder Woman's body rose from the dead!

THE GODDESS OF TRUTH

For Hera, the simplest way to resurrect Diana was to turn her into a goddess. Diana became the Goddess of Truth and took her rightful place on Mount Olympus. For a time, Hippolyta assumed the mantle of Wonder Woman. Soon, however, Diana came to feel that her true place was on Earth. Without regret, she returned to the mortal plane so that the one true Wonder Woman might continue her quest for peace.

VISIONS OF DEATH

It began in a nightmare. Hippolyta dreamed that Diana would die on Patriarch's World combating a great evil. To avoid losing her only child, Hippolyta called for a *second* contest. She also ordered the sorceress Magala to ensure Diana did not win it by casting a spell that diminished her powers—unintentionally causing Diana's death. But long before Diana's fateful end, Hippolyta confessed her duplicity, creating a deep division between mother and daughter.

WONDER QUEEN

BECAUSE HIPPOLYTA was ultimately responsible for the death of her daughter Diana and the end of Wonder Woman, the Amazon Queen felt compelled to take up the mantle herself and continue the fight to bring peace to Patriarch's World. But a battle that began in the present soon led Hippolyta to journey back in time to the year 1942, an era that had never known a Wonder Woman. Hippolyta decided to remain in the past and do her part to help end World War II and inspire a new era of peaceful coexistence among the nations of Earth. Although acting as Wonder Woman for only a short time, Hippolyta did much to uphold the ideals that Diana had lived and tragically died for.

BY COUNCIL DECREE...

When Artemis was killed fighting as Wonder Woman, Hippolyta thought that the great evil of her visions had claimed its intended victim. She was wrong. The horrific visions returned and Hippolyta glimpsed the devilish Neron. These nightmares soon came true: Diana died at Neron's hands. Hippolyta's abuse of royal power was revealed to her Amazon sisters, who decreed that their Queen should do penance by serving as Wonder Woman in Diana's place.

INTO ACTION

Wearing her own variation of Diana's Wonder Woman costume, Hippolyta arrived in Patriarch's World. First stop: the boardwalk of Gateway City. There she leaped into action alongside Donna Troy, Artemis, and Cassie Sandsmark. The heroines had to scramble Egg Fu, a teleportation machine abducting Earthlings to become slaves of Darkseid, ruler of the planet Apokolips!

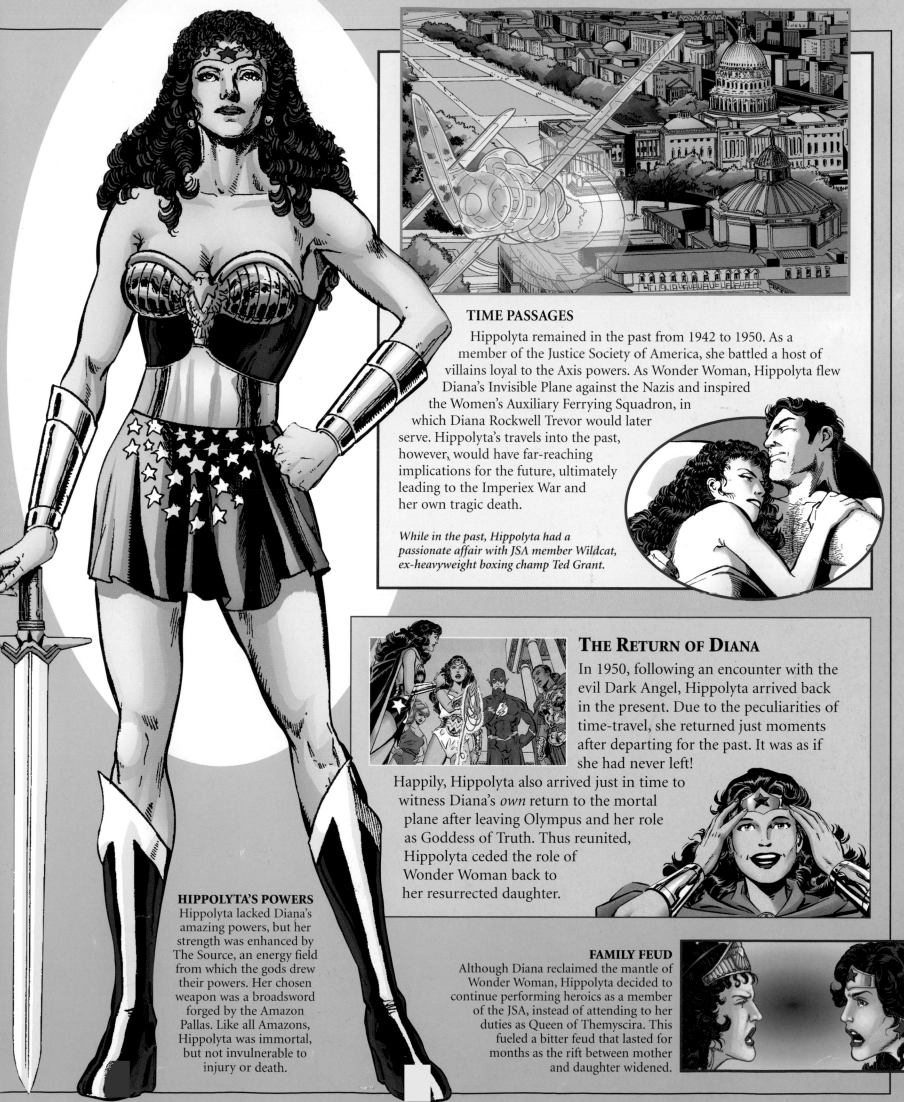

TIME PASSAGES

Hippolyta remained in the past from 1942 to 1950. As a member of the Justice Society of America, she battled a host of villains loyal to the Axis powers. As Wonder Woman, Hippolyta flew Diana's Invisible Plane against the Nazis and inspired the Women's Auxiliary Ferrying Squadron, in which Diana Rockwell Trevor would later serve. Hippolyta's travels into the past, however, would have far-reaching implications for the future, ultimately leading to the Imperiex War and her own tragic death.

While in the past, Hippolyta had a passionate affair with JSA member Wildcat, ex-heavyweight boxing champ Ted Grant.

THE RETURN OF DIANA

In 1950, following an encounter with the evil Dark Angel, Hippolyta arrived back in the present. Due to the peculiarities of time-travel, she returned just moments after departing for the past. It was as if she had never left!

Happily, Hippolyta also arrived just in time to witness Diana's *own* return to the mortal plane after leaving Olympus and her role as Goddess of Truth. Thus reunited, Hippolyta ceded the role of Wonder Woman back to her resurrected daughter.

HIPPOLYTA'S POWERS

Hippolyta lacked Diana's amazing powers, but her strength was enhanced by The Source, an energy field from which the gods drew their powers. Her chosen weapon was a broadsword forged by the Amazon Pallas. Like all Amazons, Hippolyta was immortal, but not invulnerable to injury or death.

FAMILY FEUD

Although Diana reclaimed the mantle of Wonder Woman, Hippolyta decided to continue performing heroics as a member of the JSA, instead of attending to her duties as Queen of Themyscira. This fueled a bitter feud that lasted for months as the rift between mother and daughter widened.

WARTIME HEROINE

THROUGH THE WONDERS of time travel, Queen Hippolyta helped to preserve the legacy of the Amazing Amazon years before Diana was even born! When Diana died at Neron's hands, Hippolyta donned the uniform of Wonder Woman to honor her daughter's memory. The warrior queen pursued the evil spirit Dark Angel back through history to the year 1942. There she fought alongside the Justice Society of America and helped to turn the tide against Axis aggression during World War II.

BLAST FROM THE PAST
Allied with the Justice Society's Flash, Atom, Hawkman, Johnny Thunder, and Green Lantern, Wonder Woman freed Johnny's thunderbolt from Dark Angel's thrall. Unfortunately, the evil enchantress escaped, but would bedevil Hippolyta again in 1950!

RED PANZER

To help the German war effort, Nazi scientist Helmut Streicher slipped into America in 1943 and developed a time scanner that revealed when and how the Third Reich would suffer eventual defeat. To forestall this future, Streicher forged his Red Panzer armor and attacked America's super-powered defenders, particularly Hippolyta.

ARMAGEDDON
This human juggernaut was a prime example of the Aryan supremacy Hitler hoped would prevail over America and its Allies. A Nazi "superman" whose identity was kept secret, Armageddon fought Wonder Woman for possession of mystical talismans much desired by Hitler.

BARONESS PAULA VON GUNTHER
Hippolyta's most persistent foe during the wartime years was Baroness Paula Von Gunther, a treacherous Nazi scientist. Eventually, Hippolyta defeated her and Paula was rehabilitated on Themyscira's Isle of Healing, where she devised the miraculous "Purple Healing Ray."

VILLAINY INC.

After the war, Hippolyta continued to thwart evil. In 1948, she prevented Villainy Inc. from stealing submarines moored at the Fort Church Naval Base in Virginia. The gang included Queen Clea, Princess Maru (a.k.a. Dr. Poison) The Cheetah (cat-burglar Priscilla Rich), Hypnota the Hypnotic Woman, and Zara, Mistress of the Crimson Flame.

Armed with the Trident of Poseidon and Neptune's Trumpet, Armageddon battled Hippolyta and Miss America (Diana in disguise) for the glory of the Third Reich!

ALLIED AGAINST THE AXIS

Though Hippolyta didn't realize it, *two* Wonder Women once fought side-by-side during World War II! When attempting to cross back through the dimensional barrier separating Earth from savage Skartaris, the world she had helped to liberate from Villainy Inc., Diana and Trevor Barnes accidentally emerged in the past! Fearful that she might disrupt the time-space continuum by interacting with the Wonder Woman of 1943, Diana entered the fray disguised as Miss America to battle Nazis alongside her mother!

Using her powers of transformation, Diana masqueraded as the wartime heroine known as Miss America, a disguise so perfect even her own mother was fooled!

> HIPPOLYTA.

> DIANA... SHE NEEDS YOUR HELP.

HIPPOLYTA DIES

THE IMPERIEX WAR resulted in trillions of lives lost throughout the cosmos. But none was felt more deeply by Diana and the Amazons than the death of Queen Hippolyta. She gave her life in defense of Earth, the center of the intergalactic conflict that brought the planet's greatest heroes together in an unlikely alliance with Darkseid's Apokolips and the Brainiac-controlled Warworld to halt the advance of Imperiex. In the battle to prevent the end of *everything*, Hippolyta made the ultimate sacrifice.

MOTHER TO THE RESCUE

As Imperiex-Probes assaulted Earth, Diana used the edge of her shield to pierce one robot's armor. The Imperiex-Probe exploded in a fireball that burned Wonder Woman. Hippolyta tried to comfort her injured daughter.

OFF TO BATTLE
Unable to continue the fight, Diana passed out. So Hippolyta took up her magic lasso and donned her own Amazonian battle-armor. With the Gauntlet of Atlas giving Hippolyta super-strength and the Sandals of Hermes enabling swift flight, she soared into the vacuum of space as the battle to save Earth raged on!

> DIANA!

ANGELS OF MERCY
Hippolyta's first task was to beat back the Imperiex-Probes that lay siege to the interstellar ark containing refugees from the many alien worlds already consumed in the war. Hippolyta was able to save the ark, but a greater threat loomed as one of Imperiex's machine-colony "Hollowers" fell straight towards Athens, Greece!

THE FINAL BATTLE

As Hippolyta strained to stop the Imperiex-Probe, she called upon the goddess Hera for strength to prevent the destruction of Athens, the Amazons' ancestral birthplace. Hippolyta's flesh blistered and peeled while her Amazon armor melted under the friction of reentry into Earth's atmosphere! When all seemed lost, salvation arrived as Diana rushed to Hippolyta's aid. However, another Imperiex-Probe was determined to stop both mother and daughter.

MOTHER!

NO!

KKRRRPPD

THEN I'LL SEE TO IT THAT IN THIS CREATURE'S EYES, I AM WONDER WOMAN!

EXPLOSIVE END

Hippolyta choked the Imperiex-Probe with Diana's lasso. In the ensuing explosion, the probe was destroyed. But so was a noble Wonder Woman.

BWATHOOOM

I'M SORRY, DIANA, I'M SORRY...

I'VE LOST EVERYTHING.

IMMORTAL NO MORE

Superman found Hippolyta's fallen body in a crater as fiery remnants of the Probe rained down. Diana arrived not long after. Hippolyta, scarred almost beyond recognition, was unable to speak. And as the Queen gasped her last breath, Diana spoke for both of them as she cradled her dying mother.

GREAT HERA...

MOTHER?

IT'S YOU, ISN'T IT? IT'S NOT CIRCE OR SOME DREAM—!

THANK GAEA, IT'S YOU!

LIFE AFTER DEATH

Hippolyta's body was laid to rest in a crypt within a temple erected in her honor on Themyscira's Isle of Remembrance. There, kneeling in front of a statue of Hippolyta, Diana met her mother one last time. Before Hades ushered Hippolyta into the afterlife, Hippolyta bade Diana farewell and told her daughter how proud she was of her. Joined by the spirits of Antiope and Diana Trevor, the trio of Amazon sisters reaffirmed Diana's sacred mission to transform the world in the name of peace. And with a final kiss, Hippolyta faded away forever.

ISLE OF TEACHING
Here visitors from across the universe may debate cosmic theories. Children, often orphans, are raised here by the Amazons.

REFORMATION ISLE
With its tranquil gardens and pools, even the most troubled souls, such as Paula Von Gunther and Circe, can find peace on this island devoted to the rehabilitation of evildoers.

MAIN ISLAND
The population center of Themyscira is a true "melting pot" of peoples and philosophies. Here it is possible for everyone—whether Amazon or alien—to create art and literature, and to worship their gods without fear. The tallest spire houses the official chambers of the Ministry of Themyscira, a senate of ten representatives chaired by Supreme Chancellor Phillipus, Themyscira's elected leader.

SCIENCE ISLE
Ancient ideas blend with cutting-edge technologies on this islet set aside for scientific and medical pursuits. Paula Von Gunther's "Purple Healing Ray" is based here.

WATER SYSTEM
A combination of science and sorcery keeps Themyscira aloft over the Atlantic Ocean, the waters of which are drawn up and desalinated to supply the islands' many lakes, rivers, and waterfalls.

1

THE COLISEUM

The Amazons and their Bana-Mighdall sisters practice their warrior skills in competitions that rival the Olympic games. By Aphrodite's enchantment, the Coliseum is the only place on the island chain where weapons work.

2

3

ISLE OF ASTRONOMY

This island's many telescopes blend human and alien technologies to map the heavens and scan the stars for threats such as Imperiex, Destroyer of Worlds.

1) ISLE OF HISTORY

This contains the Hall of History, a museum of the millennia, and the Library of Heroism, an archive of adventurers from Achilles to Zatanna. The latter's current curator is the super-historian known as Harbinger.

2) ISLE OF ZOOLOGY

A nature preserve for a vast variety of animal species, including the endangered dinosaurs Diana led to Themyscira from Skartaris.

3) ISLE OF REMEMBRANCE

A memorial to fallen Amazons that includes the Temple of Hippolyta erected to honor Themyscira's great leader.

NEW THEMYSCIRA

"PARADISE ISLAND" WAS LOST in the planet-shattering Imperiex War that threatened Earth with total annihilation. However Themyscira was reborn when the Olympian and Egyptian goddesses joined together to restore life to the Amazons' home and refuge. Themyscira is now a group of floating islands that utilize alien science gleaned from the WonderDome, other-dimensional energies, and a mix of ancient and modern philosophies to create a democratic society devoted to the free exchange of knowledge and the pursuit of peace.

PARADISE FOUND

New Themyscira united the Amazons with their Bana-Mighdall sisters, whose patron goddesses Isis, Mammitu, and Neith blessed the islands with magic and the spirit of motherhood. From Olympus, Demeter gave the gift of fertility, Artemis ensured game was plentiful, Hestia sanctified hearth and home, and Aphrodite gave her blessing of love and compassion.

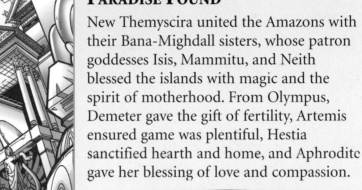

The Hall of History contains the wisdom of the ages.

Chancellor Supreme Phillipus's quarters reflect the Amazons' martial past.

The Library of Heroism records every act of valor.

Amazon and Bana-Mighdall now live side-by-side.

GLORIOUS SUNSET OVER THEMYSCIRA

Themyscira is concealed in the center of the legendary Bermuda Triangle, but it can be reached through a dimensional gateway. By the Amazons' decree, Themyscira is now a university of higher learning open to every race and gender, where visitors may study alongside the best minds in the universe.

WONDER WOMAN'S ALLIES

DIANA ALONE was chosen to carry the message of peace to Patriarch's World. But her quest has not been a lonely one. Wonder Woman's mission is championed by many. However Diana's greatest support has come from the select few fortunate enough to be counted among Diana's friends and family. In the Amazon sisterhood, Artemis of the Bana-Mighdall is one of Diana's most loyal and trusted allies, while the heroine Troia is Diana's closest living relative, a "twin" created by the devilish Dark Angel.

Some of Diana's allies are super heroes themselves: Wonder Woman remains the only permanent female member of the Justice League of America, dedicated to defending Earth from the forces of evil. However, most of Diana's closest allies are ordinary people. The first man Diana ever encountered was pilot Steve Trevor, who became Wonder Woman's first male friend. Julia and Vanessa Kapatelis befriended Diana when she first journeyed to Patriarch's World.

Detective Mike Schorr was just one of many new acquaintances Wonder Woman made in California's Gateway City. Mike's feelings for Diana ran deeper than friendship: the same might be said for Trevor Barnes, whose love for Diana may not be so unrequited! Also among Diana's personal ties to Gateway City were museum curator Helena Sandsmark and her daughter Cassie.

Whether Wonder Woman's friends and allies are endowed with superpowers or ordinary humans, all are ready to fight alongside Diana, inspired by her timeless spirit and her commitment to truth and liberty!

ARTEMIS

AFTER HIPPOLYTA and Diana, Artemis is the only other Amazon worthy of the title "Wonder Woman." A member of the Bana-Mighdall tribe, Artemis won the contest to select a new Wonder Woman, besting Diana in the process! Unfortunately, Artemis died soon after and was exiled to Hades. Diana helped Artemis to escape the underworld and the two grew to respect one another. Artemis is the chief warrior, or "Shim'Tar," of the Bana-Mighdall, and is pledged to defend New Themyscira as one of Wonder Woman's most trusted allies.

Artemis is deadly with a sword, yet prefers a bow and arrow to other weapons.

Artemis has mastered many forms of ancient and modern combat.

THE CONTEST

Visions of Diana's death spurred Queen Hippolyta to call for a new contest to choose another ambassador to Patriarch's World. Hippolyta knew that her daughter was more than a match for any Amazon, so she ordered the sorceress Magala to transfer a portion of Diana's might to her closest competitor. Thus empowered, Artemis won the contest, racing to victory while Diana fell behind, saving other participants from monsters like the Medusa and Charybdis.

A FIERY NEW WONDER WOMAN

In addition to taking up Diana's tiara and lasso, Artemis was awarded two other talismans to help her carry the Amazons' message of peace to Patriarch's World. The Gauntlet of Atlas increased her strength tenfold, while the Sandals of Hermes gave her the power of swift flight.

REAL NAME Artemis
OCCUPATION Adventurer
BASE New Themyscira
HEIGHT 6 ft 1 in
WEIGHT 140 lb
EYES Blue HAIR Red
FIRST APPEARANCE
WONDER WOMAN vol. 2 #90
(September 1994)

Like the rest of her Bana-Mighdall sisters, Artemis was enchanted with immortality by Circe.

REQUIEM FOR ARTEMIS

Artemis wore the official mantle of the Amazing Amazon, but Diana was still regarded as the one true Wonder Woman. Artemis vowed to prove her mettle and set out to clean up organized crime in Boston. This brought her into conflict with the White Magician. Impetuous Artemis underestimated the White Magician's might and died battling him. She was consigned to Hades, where she became the unwilling bride of Dalkriig-Hath, a prince of the underworld. Ultimately, Diana would be her salvation.

THE HELLENDERS

With Diana's help, Artemis escaped Hades and returned to the mortal world. She adopted the name Requiem for a time and joined the Hellenders, a team of monster hunters. Her teammates included Shock Treatment, Sojourner, Deadfall, and Sureshot. Tragically, her fellow Hellenders Spiral, Corrode, Warhammer, Rewind, and Download were killed by her own demon husband, Dalkriig-Hath.

OUT OF THE INFERNAL DEPTHS

Death and resurrection have changed Artemis's headstrong ways. When the demon Neron captured her, Wonder Woman, and Helena and Cassie Sandsmark, Artemis patiently braided a rope from her own hair to escape the fiery pits of Neron's hellish realm.

TEACHER AND MENTOR

When Helena Sandsmark forbade Wonder Woman from teaching Helena's daughter Cassie to master her godly powers, Diana asked Artemis to serve as Cassie's mentor. Artemis lived in Gateway City for almost a year while she trained the young Wonder Girl in the ways of the Amazon warriors.

TROIA

DONNA TROY is Diana's adopted sister, the *second* princess of Themyscira! She began as Diana's identical twin, but was kidnapped and reincarnated many times. In her final incarnation she was Troy, an orphan child raised on the planet New Chronus by the Titans of Myth. With 12 other children she was to become one of a new race of gods! However Donna returned to Earth and adopted the alter ego "Wonder Girl," inspired by Hippolyta, the Wonder Woman of the 1940s. Donna later changed her name to "Troia" to reflect her godly heritage. She also learned that she was actually created from a fragment of Diana's own soul!

MIRROR IMAGE
As the only child on Themyscira, Diana longed for a playmate, so the sorceress Magala brought Diana's own reflection to life!

THE MANY LIVES OF DONNA

The devilish Dark Angel spirited away Diana's "twin" and used her evil magicks to make Diana's reflection suffer a series of tortured and tragic lives. But every time the twin was resurrected, its fragment of Diana's soul *changed*. Inadvertently, Dark Angel created a whole new person separate and distinct from Diana, the woman eventually called Donna Troy!

REAL NAME
Donna Hinckley Stacey Troy

OCCUPATION
Photographer; adventurer

BASE New York City

HEIGHT 5 ft 9 in **WEIGHT** 125 lb

EYES Blue **HAIR** Black

FIRST APPEARANCE
THE BRAVE AND THE BOLD #60
(June–July 1965)

ALWAYS A HEROINE

Aged 13, Donna became the teen heroine Wonder Girl. She soon joined the Teen Titans alongside Robin, Speedy, Kid Flash, and Aqualad, later altering her codename and costume. Donna lost her godly abilities and joined the Darkstars, a corps of intergalactic peacekeepers. She resumed her heroic role as Troia after the Darkstars were disbanded and her powers restored.

As Wonder Girl

As a Darkstar

As Troia

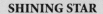

SHINING STAR

Troia's costume is a design based on her second Wonder Girl costume, yet incorporating the miraculous "star-field" fabric—a gift from the Titans of Myth—that shines with stellar light. Troia's uniform is also a stellar map pinpointing the exact location of New Chronus.

MARRIAGE AND TRAGEDY

Amazons, Teen Titans, and mortals were among the guests when Donna married longtime love Terry Long. Donna's teammate Starfire was her bridesmaid and Dick Grayson, her closest friend, walked her down the aisle. Sadly, the marriage was not to last, soon ending in divorce, despite the birth of their son, Robert. Tragically, both ex-husband and son were killed not long after in a car crash.

TROY, SPARTA, AND ATHEYNS

Donna was drawn back to New Chronus when fellow orphan Sparta of Synriannaq sought to destroy the other eleven children—now grown to adulthood—and claim their godly powers for herself. With her New Titans teammates beside her, Donna and her "brother" Atheyns defeated Sparta and saved the Titans of Myth. Following this adventure, Donna adopted the name "Troia" to reflect her true heritage.

SKILLS AND POWERS

Donna learned martial arts on New Chronus. As a Teen Titan, she refined her skills by sparring with Princess Koriand'r of Tamaran, a.k.a. Starfire, once a pupil of the Warlords of Okaara. Troia's powers include super-strength and speed, flight, and a psychic link with Diana. Like her sister, Donna also has the power to elicit the truth from most people.

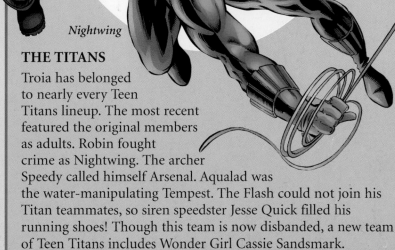

Troia

Tempest

Arsenal

Jesse Quick

Nightwing

THE TITANS

Troia has belonged to nearly every Teen Titans lineup. The most recent featured the original members as adults. Robin fought crime as Nightwing. The archer Speedy called himself Arsenal. Aqualad was the water-manipulating Tempest. The Flash could not join his Titan teammates, so siren speedster Jesse Quick filled his running shoes! Though this team is now disbanded, a new team of Teen Titans includes Wonder Girl Cassie Sandsmark.

FURY

Tisiphone, the Blood Avenger.

Helena as Fury.

REAL NAME Helena Kosmatos
OCCUPATION Adventurer
BASE New Themyscira
HEIGHT 5 ft 6 in
WEIGHT 118 lb
EYES Blue **HAIR** Blonde
FIRST APPEARANCE
SECRET ORIGINS vol. 2 #12
(March 1987)

A CRY OF RAGE and a shouted curse gave Helena Kosmatos the power to avenge the murder of her mother. When Helena's brother Michael collaborated with the Axis powers in 1941 against their Greek countrymen, the shock of Michael's betrayal caused their mother to suffer a fatal heart attack. Helena blamed Michael for her death and fled to the Aeropagus, Ares's lair, where she cursed Michael's name. There, Helena met the trio of Furies, merciless spirits of vengeance. With a touch, Helena became host to Tisiphone the Blood Avenger, who would empower Helena to become the feared wartime heroine known as Fury!

FURY'S POWERS

Possessed by the spirit of Tisiphone, Fury has superhuman strength and speed, and wears lightweight, bulletproof, golden armor. She can also transform into flying "Blood Avenger" form with enhanced abilities, and the power to project heat beams from her eyes. In 1942, Fury helped the All-Star Squadron of super heroes defeat Axis Amerika, a group of superpowered enemy agents. Fury later joined the Young All-Stars in training.

YOU WILL NOT TAKE EVERYTHING FROM ME!!!

BOOM

SIBLING RIVALRY
During World War II, Helena became friends with Queen Hippolyta in her role as Wonder Woman. After marrying and giving birth to a daughter, Helena named the child after Hippolyta, whom she had wrongly come to regard as her own mother, magically reincarnated. Years later, Fury met Diana—with explosive results!

ACCEPTING THE TRUTH
Diana's love of truth and Helena's delusion that Hippolyta was her own mother put the pair on a collision course. However, sympathy replaced anger in Diana's heart, and she brought Helena to Hippolyta, who said that she was Helena's mother "in every way that matters."

AMAZONS AT WAR

When Hippolyta left Themyscira to serve as Wonder Woman, Fury came under the dangerous influence of the Amazon sorceress Magala—instigator of the bloody civil conflict between the Amazons and their Bana-Mighdall sisters. Magala manipulated Helena's lingering jealousy of Diana and her hatred of Hippolyta's enemies to turn Fury into her own personal weapon of war.

BLOOD GIFT
As civil war raged, Magala tried to depose Hippolyta. That was a fatal mistake. Fury—turned Blood Avenger—tore out Magala's heart, and offered it to Hippolyta.

HELP ME!

FOR HIPPOLYTA!
Following the murder of Magala, Hippolyta and the surviving Amazons took on the task of healing Helena's fractured mind. But when Hippolyta fell in battle during the Imperiex War, Fury's demand for vengeance could not be contained. The Blood Avenger soared into Earth's orbit and tore into the Imperiex-Probes that had killed her surrogate mother.

A TROUBLED SPIRIT
After Hippolyta's tragic death, Helena's mental state was further undermined when Angle Man stole an ancient talisman that allowed Barbara Minerva to take possession of the spirit of Tisiphone and use the Fury's powers to fight Sébastian Ballesteros for control of the Cheetah! Helena lay near death until the bitter battle between Minerva and Ballesteros was resolved. Ballesteros remained the Cheetah, while Minerva vanished. Tisiphone, meanwhile, returned to inhabit Helena's troubled soul once more.

THE TREVORS

Hippolyta's adventures as Wonder Woman aboard her Invisible Plane inspired Diana Trevor to become a pilot.

THE DESTINIES OF DIANA Rockwell Trevor and her son Steve are intertwined with the Amazons of Themyscira and Wonder Woman. When she crashed her plane on the island paradise in 1945, pilot Diana Trevor gave her life to save a host of Amazons battling creatures loosed from Doom's Doorway. Queen Hippolyta named her daughter after the heroic aviatrix. Many years later later, Diana Trevor's son, U.S. Air Force Colonel Steve Trevor, became the first mortal man ever to set foot on Themyscira.

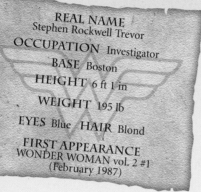

REAL NAME
Stephen Rockwell Trevor

OCCUPATION Investigator

BASE Boston

HEIGHT 6 ft 1 in

WEIGHT 195 lb

EYES Blue HAIR Blond

FIRST APPEARANCE
WONDER WOMAN vol. 2 #1
(February 1987)

PENTAGON CORRUPTION

Steve Trevor had a highly successful career in the U. S. Air Force until he testified before Congress during an investigation into corruption at the Pentagon. Honest and loyal, he was branded a snitch by his military peers and assigned a desk job under General Gerard Kohler, an agent of Ares.

THE LOST PLANE

Kohler ordered Colonel Trevor to fly the Air Force's newly modified Phantom fighter jet on a demonstration bombing run inside the Bermuda Triangle. Little did Steve know that the island of Themyscira was his target. Spying the Amazons' refuge, Steve refused to drop his bomb; then he discovered that his co-pilot, Capt. Slade, was a demonic minion of Ares! Steve and Slade fought for control of the plane, which spiraled into the Atlantic. Meanwhile Wonder Woman lassoed the Phantom's bomb and saved Themyscira from a fiery doom.

After the Amazons nursed Steve back to health, he went with Diana on her first journey to Patriarch's World.

ETTA CANDY TREVOR

U. S. Air Force Lieutenant Etta Candy was one of Wonder Woman's first trusted allies in Patriarch's World. During the "Ares Affair" when the war god threatened Earth with atomic annihilation, Etta helped to clear Steve Trevor's name after U. S. military personnel loyal to Ares branded him a traitor. Steve and Etta's friendship turned to love as the years went by and the two became husband and wife. Steve is now retired from active duty, while Etta has been promoted to the rank of captain.

Diana was one of Etta's bridesmaids at her wedding to Steve Trevor. It took place in Oklahoma, close to Trevor's only living relatives.

REAL NAME Etta Candy Trevor

OCCUPATION
U. S. Air Force Captain,

BASE Boston

HEIGHT 5 ft 3 in

WEIGHT 135 lb

EYES Brown **HAIR** Brown

FIRST APPEARANCE
WONDER WOMAN vol. 2 #2
(March 1987)

ETTA'S ANOREXIA

When she first met the beautiful Diana, Etta was jealous of Wonder Woman's rapport with Steve Trevor. Although she soon came to admire the Amazon Princess and develop a close friendship with her, she was secretly envious of Diana's svelte figure. She developed an eating disorder that threatened her life. Diana discovered that poor Etta had been starving herself to stay thin, and convinced her that beauty was more than skin deep.

THE TREVORS IN PARADISE

Years before their wedding, Steve Trevor and Etta Candy visited Themyscira as guests of the grateful Amazons. In the Temple of Hades, Steve stood before the statue erected to Diana Trevor, and confessed aloud his pent-up feelings of abandonment by his mother, who had left him on a Christmas Eve so many years before to fly on her final fateful mission. Steve is always welcome to return to Themyscira whenever he wishes to visit Diana Trevor's tomb and remember his own personal Wonder Woman.

THE KAPATELIS FAMILY

AS IF BY FATE, Wonder Woman's first female friend in Patriarch's World was Julia Kapatelis, a woman with secret, surprisingly close ties to Themyscira. As an archaeologist and a professor of Greek culture, Julia was perhaps the best possible person to guide the Amazon Princess as she adjusted to the language and customs of her new home in America. Diana found herself once more part of a family of strong, capable women as she became a sister to Julia's daughter Vanessa. No one could have known that Vanessa would one day be tragically transformed into Diana's foe!

JULIA'S HOME
Julia Kapatelis lived in one of the handsome, red brick, three-story houses common to Boston's prestigious Beacon Hill district. During much of her time in Boston, Wonder Woman lived with the Kapatelis family here. The home was frequently remodeled owing to the demands of living with a super-strong Amazon Princess.

FIRST MEETING

Diana was conveyed to Patriarch's World by Hermes the Messenger God. To help her adapt to life among mankind, Hermes took her to Harvard University to meet Professor Julia Kapatelis. As Julia tumbled off a high ladder in one of Harvard's libraries, Diana caught her! Julia, of Greek descent herself, swiftly mastered Diana's Amazon dialect and taught Wonder Woman English.

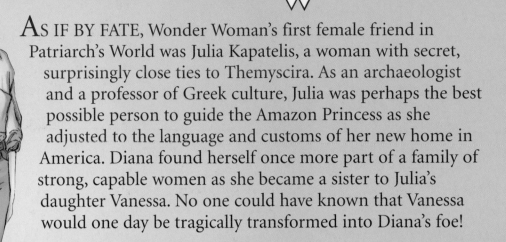

REAL NAME Julia Kapatelis
OCCUPATION Professor of Archaeology and Greek Culture
BASE Boston
HEIGHT 5 ft 3 in
WEIGHT 140 lb
EYES Blue HAIR Blonde
FIRST APPEARANCE
WONDER WOMAN vol. 2 #3
(April 1987)

BURIED MEMORIES

Not even Julia herself realized that she had once spent time on Themyscira! As an infant, Julia—who was born in Cephalonia, Greece—fell overboard from her father Agostos's fishing boat and was rescued by the Neriedes. These water-dwelling nymphs carried Julia to the shores of Themyscira, where the Amazon Phthia instilled in her the Themysciran ideals of love and equality. Phthia then safely returned little Julia to her father's boat, turning back time so that Julia's fall from it never happened.

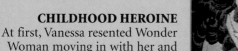

AN IMPRESSIONABLE CHILD

Vanessa Kapatelis is the only child of Julia Kapatelis and her husband David, also a noted archaeologist. David died when Vanessa was only five years old. The loss of Vanessa's father would prove to be a crucial moment in her life, the first of many tragedies that would transform her from a well-adjusted teenager into an emotionally scarred young woman, easily manipulated into becoming a tool of vengeance for one of Wonder Woman's most diabolical enemies, Circe!

CHILDHOOD HEROINE

At first, Vanessa resented Wonder Woman moving in with her and her mother on Beacon Hill. When Julia went away on archaeological digs, Vanessa used to stay with other family members. She jealously guarded time spent alone with her mother and felt Diana was an intruder. However, Vanessa gradually came to love and admire Diana as the older sister she would never have.

The suicide of her best friend, Lucy Spears, had a traumatic emotional effect on Vanessa that would haunt her for ever.

A TROUBLED TEENAGER

Vanessa's connection to Wonder Woman brought her happiness *and* horror. After the Trevors, Vanessa and her mother were the first outsiders to visit Themyscira, making the high-school student something of a celebrity. But being Diana's "little sister" also made Vanessa the target of Wonder Woman's foes, including Decay and Dr. Psycho. Decay once terrifyingly aged Vanessa's body, while Dr. Psycho inflicted lasting damage on her mind. The suicide of one friend and the death of another also threatened Vanessa's mental state.

As her family and friends searched for clues to Vanessa's metamorphosis into the hate-filled Silver Swan, Cassie Sandsmark discovered a diary detailing Vanessa's horrifying descent into madness.

VANESSA'S SWAN SONG

When Diana left, Vanessa felt abandoned by her longtime friend. Close to despair, she allowed herself to be transformed into the second Silver Swan. When Diana returned to Boston in an effort to understand Vanessa's transformation, Julia couldn't help but blame Wonder Woman for allowing her daughter to become yet another pawn of Circe. Diana promised to do whatever she could to bring Vanessa back from the brink of insanity.

COAST TO COAST

DIANA KNEW that the duties of Wonder Woman meant leaving the peace and seclusion of Themyscira and living as a stranger in the strange land the Amazons called "Patriarch's World." The prospect did not seem particularly inviting, but Diana duly departed her Amazon sisters, bound for the U. S. and its great cities. The country's belief in democracy and freedom gave Wonder Woman hope that the realm of mankind might yet be redeemed.

WELCOME TO BOSTON

Of all the cities she has called home, Diana has lived longest in Boston, Massachusetts. Diana met Julia and Vanessa Kapatelis, who welcomed the Amazon Princess into their home and made her feel part of the family. Here also, Diana was introduced to publicist Myndi Mayer. She organized a public relations tour introducing Diana to the world after the press dubbed her "Wonder Woman" following her defeat of Ares and his plans to bring about nuclear armageddon.

GATEWAY CITY

Diana traded the Atlantic coast for the Pacific when she moved to California's Gateway City. Following the death of Artemis, Diana needed a change of scenery. The warm climate of Gateway City, regarded as one of the ten greatest cities in the world, seemed like the perfect environment to forget the woes she left behind in Boston. With no resident hero to call its own, Gateway welcomed Wonder Woman with open arms.

DET. MIKE SCHORR

Although he would have preferred to be *more* than just a friend, Diana's most trusted ally in Gateway City was G. C. P. D. Officer Mike Schorr, a young but highly decorated lawman. Officer Schorr was often the first policeman on the scene whenever Wonder Woman battled supervillains in defense of her new home.

HELENA SANDSMARK

Gateway City Museum of Cultural Antiquities Director Helena Sandsmark hired Diana as a visiting lecturer in Greco-Roman Mythology. Having Wonder Woman on staff has endangered the museum's exhibits, and her presence has inspired Helena's daughter Cassie to become the super hero Wonder Girl; nevertheless Helena has found her friendship with the Amazon Princess rewarding.

On her very first day at the museum, Diana faced a squad of ancient warriors loosed from a 10th-century tapestry and a reactivated battle-robot!

YOU'LL BE CLOSE ENOUGH TO WORK AND WE CAN *HANG OUT* AND EAT ICE CREAM AND WATCH MOVIES AND *DISH MEN.* C'MON, SIS!

WHAT DO YOU THINK?

HOW COULD I POSSIBLY SAY "NO" TO ALL THAT?

I'D *LOVE* TO BE YOUR ROOMMATE.

FROM WASHINGTON TO NEW YORK

For a short time, Diana resided in Washington, D. C., where her mother had based herself while serving as Wonder Woman during World War II, and for several years afterwards. Diana's home at this time was the magical WonderDome, an embassy of peace that floated in the sky above the U. S. capital! Diana later relocated to New York City, where she stayed with her sister Donna Troy in Donna's penthouse apartment.

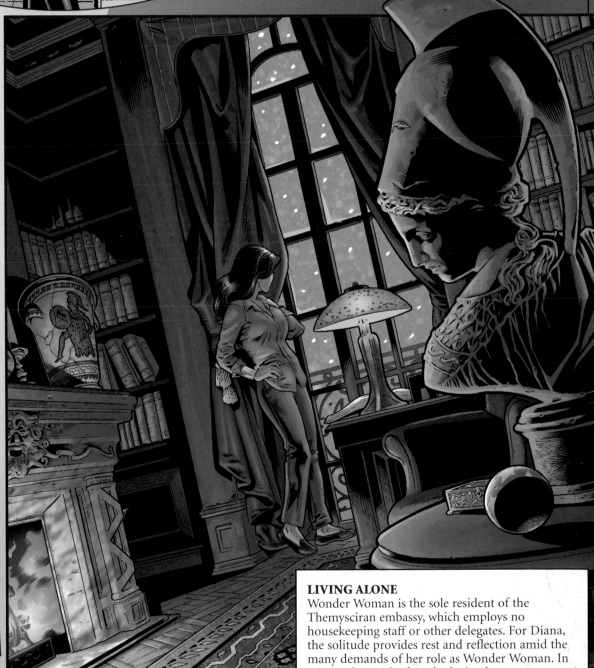

EMBASSY SUITE

Diana now resides at the Embassy of Themyscira in Manhattan. Her role as the Amazon ambassador to Patriarch's World sometimes requires her to speak before the United Nation's General Assembly. Living in New York City gives Diana ample opportunity to champion the cause of peace.

A HOUSE OF SANCTUARY

Themyscira House is situated near Central Park. Its façade has columns carved from Themysciran marble and it contains many fine examples of Amazon arts and crafts. The embassy offers sanctuary to anyone in need of protection.

LIVING ALONE

Wonder Woman is the sole resident of the Themysciran embassy, which employs no housekeeping staff or other delegates. For Diana, the solitude provides rest and reflection amid the many demands of her role as Wonder Woman. In winter, she can be found relaxing by an open fire—even a Wonder Woman sometimes feels homesick for the tropical breezes of her birthplace.

WONDER GIRL

UNLIKE THE TROJAN prophetess of Greek legend she is named after, Cassandra Sandsmark was not able to see into the future. So she never knew how fateful would prove the day when she first took up the Gauntlet of Atlas and the Sandals of Hermes to help her friend and mentor Wonder Woman. Her role as "Wonder Girl" continued long after she had acquired her own god-given powers, and she trained hard to become an Amazon warrior and a super heroine in her own right!

A GOD'S GIFTS

Impressed by Cassie's youthful courage, Zeus empowered her with flight and super-strength. He also gave Cassie's mother Helena the ability to remove her daughter's powers for one hour simply by touching her!

CASSIE, IT'S ME! YOU'VE GOT TO BREAK THIS SPELL... GET DEVASTATION OUT OF YOUR HEAD!

HER EYES... I KNOW SHE'S SEEING SOMETHING ELSE.

I'VE SHOWN YOU FOR THE BABY YOU REALLY ARE! YOU'RE A LITTLE GIRL, NOT READY FOR A WOMAN'S WORLD!

A WORTHY HEROINE

Diana and Artemis schooled the new Wonder Girl in all of the Amazons' martial skills. Cassie demonstrated her worthiness to wear Amazon bracelets when she refused to let herself become Devastation's mind-controlled puppet and battle Wonder Woman to the death!

YOUNG JUSTICE

Wonder Girl once belonged to Young Justice, a teenaged super-hero team including Superboy, Robin, and Impulse (pictured). Young Justice disbanded when many of its members——Cassie among them——joined a new assembly of Teen Titans mentored by Troia's former teammates Beast Boy, Cyborg, and Starfire.

REAL NAME
Cassandra "Cassie" Sandsmark

OCCUPATION High-school student

BASE Gateway City, CA

HEIGHT 5 ft 1 in

WEIGHT 105 lb

EYES Blue **HAIR** Blonde

FIRST APPEARANCE
WONDER WOMAN vol. 2 #105
(February 1996)

HIGH-SCHOOL CONFIDENTIAL

At first Cassie wore a black wig and goggles to mask her identity as Wonder Girl. Soon, a wish for more fashionable fighting togs led Cassie to ditch this disguise. However, when the crazed Silver Swan reduced Cassie's Gateway City high school to rubble with her shattering scream, Cassie revealed her secret identity to the world by helping to save her classmates!

THE ULTIMATE FATHER

Cassie had never known her father's identity. She suspected that it might be Zeus, but the god denied it. Then Cassie met a man from Portland, Oregon, who claimed to be her father. Cassie didn't suspect that this normal-looking man was Zeus in disguise!

THE JLA

THE JUSTICE LEAGUE OF AMERICA is a select group of the world's greatest super heroes gathered together to thwart tyranny. While many of Earth's costumed champions are auxiliary members of the JLA, the team's core membership is Superman, Batman, Wonder Woman, Aquaman, Martian Manhunter, Flash, Green Lantern, and Plastic Man. Based in a gleaming citadel called The Watchtower on the surface of the Moon, the JLA stands as Earth's *best* defense against any threat.

> ⟨QUICKLY MY FRIEND, QUICKLY.⟩

SCH ZOMM

THE OBSIDIAN AGE
During the Imperiex War, Aquaman saved Atlantis by hurling the city 3,000 years into the past. When the citizens faced enslavement by super-beings the Ancients, the JLA embarked on a time-traveling rescue mission. Green Lantern, riding on a power-ring-generated giant tabby cat, helped free Wonder Woman from the Ancients' Manitou Raven and the armored warrior Montezumak.

THE GOLDEN PERFECT
On one JLA mission, Wonder Woman's faith in herself and her beliefs were tested by the mystical Rama Khan, whose magicks shredded the Lasso of Hestia and unraveled the fabric of truth binding reality together. Diana's quest to mend her golden lariat took her to the Land of Shade where she battled mythical monsters before defeating Rama Khan himself!

DEATH AND THE MAIDEN
The Justice League members always stand by one another, but when the devilish Neron felled Diana, her male compatriots were powerless to revive her! As Diana's vital signs dwindled, the helpless JLA mourned her passing.

GREEN LANTERN
Kyle Rayner is the last Green Lantern. Kyle wields an Oan power ring that can convert his every thought into tangible green energy.

BATMAN
As a boy, Bruce Wayne witnessed the brutal slayings of his parents. Since then he has devoted his life to fighting crime.

SUPERMAN
Superman's powers are fueled by Earth's yellow sun. He is Earth's mightiest hero and the JLA's moral center.

WONDER WOMAN
The lone woman amid the core team, Diana is as strong as the League's mightiest members, Superman and Martian Manhunter.

FLASH
Wally West was endowed with super-speed after a freak laboratory accident. Once a Teen Titan alongside Donna Troy, Wally has since graduated to the *big* League.

MARTIAN MANHUNTER
J'onn J'onzz is the sole survivor of a Green Martian race devastated by a plague. His powers include shapeshifting, telepathy, super-strength, flight, and "Martian Vision."

AQUAMAN
Of all Diana's teammates, the monarch Aquaman is perhaps furthest from her in philosophy and temperament, despite their respective royal upbringings. Orin of Atlantis was recently stripped of his crown, but he remains a devoted defender of Earth's oceans.

PLASTIC MAN
After a dunking in acid made his body as resilient as rubber, gangster Eel O'Brian changed his wicked ways and used his new pliant powers as Plastic Man!

WONDER WOMEN

WONDER WOMAN'S STRENGTH and wisdom have made her a shining example to other super heroines. However, Wonder Woman's inspiration is not confined to the good deeds of Princess Diana. It also includes the brave exploits of her mother Hippolyta, who took on the role of Wonder Woman when Diana "died" at the hands of demon Neron. Hippolyta time-travelled back to 1943 to combat the Nazis, while her young daughter Diana was growing up in blissful innocence on Themyscira. So future heroines have been inspired by both Diana *and* Hippolyta to become "wonder women!"

SUPERGIRL

When the artificial life form known as Supergirl saved artist Linda Danvers's life, the two merged into a single being dedicated to protecting the innocent, just like her "cousin" and inspiration Superman! Once possessing fiery angelic wings, Supergirl can no longer fly, but instead is able to leap approximately one-eighth of a mile. Her strength, however, remains quite formidable.

GIRL POWER!

The enchantress Circe once transformed Earth's male super heroes into were-creatures and loosed an army of villainesses to hunt them down in the concrete jungle of Manhattan. Fortunately, Wonder Woman mustered every available super heroine to stop Circe's legion of lethal ladies!

LOIS LANE

Although she has no super-powers to call her own, intrepid reporter Lois Lane has made a career out of risking her life to get the big story. Unknown to the world-at-large, Lois is married to Superman. Lois is one of Diana's closest friends despite the fact that Wonder Woman once dated the Man of Steel when he was a bachelor!

ZATANNA

She may dress like a stage magician, but Zatanna Zatara is a powerful sorceress and an auxiliary member of the JLA. The daughter of "Mystery Man" John Zatara and the sorceress Sindella, a member of the mystical *Homo magi* race, Zatanna wields powerful magic by speaking her spells *sdrawkcab* (backwards)!

HAWKGIRL

Kendra Saunders is the reincarnation of Egyptian Princess Chay-Ara. The souls of the princess and her lover Prince Khufu were transformed by the power source from a crashed spacecraft from the planet Thanagar. The couple became the high-flying Hawkgirl and Hawkman, heroes destined to be reborn life after life to rekindle their love and battle evil where they find it.

A WARRIOR'S WEAPONS

With her preference for ancient weapons, such as her spiked mace, curved Kris dagger, and sharp-knuckled cestuses, Hawkgirl would feel at home on Themyscira's Coliseum Island.

POWER GIRL

A daughter of doomed Atlantis, Kara was saved from death, granted magical abilities, and sent forward in time by her grandfather, Arion. Kara's "Power Girl" was a member of Justice League Europe during Diana's brief association with the team. However she is best known as a member of the Justice Society as the legendary team's strongest muscle.

BATGIRL

A trained assassin from infancy, Cassandra Cain is still learning what it means to be a super-heroine, even though she may well be the greatest living martial artist, perhaps even rivaling her mentor the Dark Knight!

SCREAM QUEEN

A metahuman by birth, Black Canary possesses a hypersonic "Canary Cry," a high-pitched shriek of amazing power that can shred metal or literally knock opponents off their feet.

BLACK CANARY

Dinah Lance and Diana share a common background. Both of their mothers belonged to the Justice Society of America during World War II! Dinah's mother was the original Black Canary, known for her fishnet stockings and leather, as well as her judo black belt. Dinah co-founded the Justice League, but now continues in her mother's role as a member of the JSA.

GODLY AVATARS

THE HINDU TRIMURTI
In the Hindu pantheon, the Trimurti are three gods that encompass all of time and space and are the manifestation of Brahman, the universal spirit flowing through creation. Brahma (center) is the creator of all things. Vishnu (left) maintains the life of creation. Most feared among the trio is Shiva (right), the destroyer god, who ends the cycle of life.

SINCE THE DAWN of creation, gods have come and gone. Some are distant memories; others, like the Olympic and Hindu pantheons, are blessed with loyal followers devoted to their powers and principles. Each divine presence has its champion. Wonder Woman shares a portion of her powers with Captain Marvel. Black Adam draws his abilities from little-known Egyptian deities. The Son of Vulcan died defending the gods who empowered him. Still others exist as agents of order or of chaos.

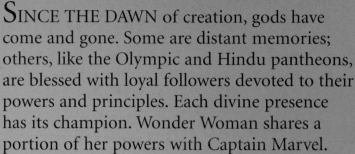

BLACK ADAM
When he discovered an ancient amulet, ruthless Theo Adam became possessed by the powers and memories of the Egyptian hero-turned-villain Black Adam. This spirit, created by the wizard Shazam, seeks to redeem himself and fights a constant struggle with Theo Adam to remain good, a cause supported by Black Adam's fellow members in the JSA.

CAPTAIN MARVEL
With a single magic word—Shazam!—young Billy Batson turns into Captain Marvel! When Billy's archaeologist parents were killed by their associate Theo Adam, Billy worked as a newsboy and slept in the subway. One night, Billy was led to a cavern, where he met the wizard Shazam. He was chosen to be the wizard's successor in the fight against evil and given the wisdom of Solomon, the strength of Hercules, the power of Zeus, the courage of Achilles, and the speed of Mercury. Billy became one of the greatest champions the world has ever known.

THE QUINTESSENCE

The Quintessence is a council of five sage immortals that watches over over the course of mankind's evolution. The Olympian Zeus needs no introduction. The wizard Shazam has been fighting evil since ancient Egyptian times. Clad in his trenchcoat and fedora, the Phantom Stranger is an enigma, yet always appears in times of dire need. The staff-wielding Highfather once led the New Gods of New Genesis away from marauding Darkseid and his minions on Apokolips. Lastly, the blue-skinned Ganthet is the sole surviving Guardian of the Universe, a being older than time who helped to create and fuel the vaunted Green Lantern Corps as galactic peacekeepers.

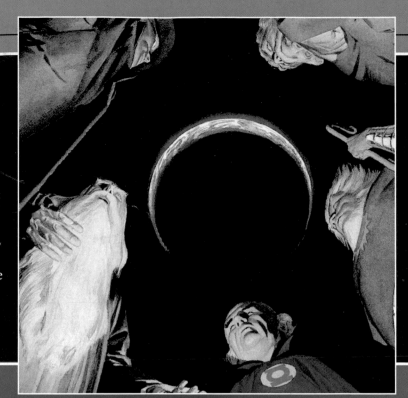

SON OF VULCAN

While covering a civil war on the Mediterranean island of Cyprete, disillusioned reporter Johnny Mann shouted a challenge to the Roman gods. Mann was struck by lightning and transported to the gods' heavenly home. Though many of the gods desired Mann's execution for his pride, Vulcan spared his life and granted him godly powers to battle evil.

DOCTOR FATE

He is an Agent of Order, charged by the sorcerer Nabu to be Earth's defender. Archaeologist Kent Nelson was the first to wield the magical might within the helm and amulet of Nabu as Dr. Fate. Hector Hall, once the hero Silver Scarab, now possesses Fate's powers.

WAR OF THE GODS

In ages past, gods have fought for dominion over mankind, but none of these conflicts rivaled the tumult unleashed by the sorceress Circe in her scheme to destroy Gaea herself. This "War of the Gods" set pantheon against pantheon and champion against champion with the fate of reality at stake. As Greek gods fought their Roman counterparts, Wonder Woman battled her heroic peer Captain Marvel, and Black Adam led an army of supervillains against Circe.

FRIENDS AND LOVED ONES

DIANA IS FIERCELY LOYAL to her friends and to those she loves. On Themyscira, Diana had close ties to many of her Amazon sisters. In Patriarch's World, she overcame being a stranger among strangers and found a core group of comrades who quickly became a substitute family for her. Raised to be caring and compassionate, Diana is not afraid to love deeply and without the expectation of her affection being returned. She is also unashamed to openly express her feelings for others. Diana's great empathy and her tolerance for all beliefs make her the *best friend* that anyone could ever dream of.

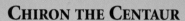

CHIRON THE CENTAUR

The noble centaur Chiron was one of several mythological creatures—including the riddle-spinning Sphynx, the winged steed Pegasus, and the chess-loving dragon Ladon—who inhabited Wonder Woman's previous WonderDome headquarters. Chiron was a master archer and the wisest of this quartet of "advisors." Chiron's natural gifts in the healing arts saved Diana's life on several occasions.

MYNDI MAYER

Celebrity publicist Myndi Mayer exploited her charms to the full and didn't care whose toes she stepped on in her all-consuming drive for success. During Diana's first year in Patriarch's World, Myndi orchestrated the nationwide Wonder Woman Tour, a public relations campaign to help the Amazon Princess spread Themyscira's message of peace and equality. Myndi helped make Wonder Woman a household name, but accidentally overdosed on cocaine. Her death was initially believed to have been murder.

ED INDELICATO

Boston Police Inspector Ed Indelicato met Wonder Woman when she fought the first Silver Swan (Valerie Beaudry). His detective work helped unravel the details of Myndi Mayer's death. Indelicato had a crush on Diana while she was in Boston, but he later fell in love with Myndi Mayer's sister Wendy after he and Diana cured her of an addiction to the drug Lethe.

JULIA THE DAXAMITE

When the White Magician cast Diana into deep space, one of the aliens she encountered was a fierce Daxamite female. After Diana demonstrated her fighting prowess the Daxamite—whom Diana dubbed "Julia" after Julia Kapatelis—befriended the Amazon Princess. Like Superman, Julia possessed incredible superpowers under the light of a yellow sun.

MIKE SCHORR

Gateway City cop Mike Schorr was also infatuated with the Amazon Princess. When Diana told Mike she did not share his feelings, the two stayed friends. Mike's devotion did not diminish, and he continued to help Diana during some of the worst times in her life. Mike fought bravely beside Diana when Darkseid invaded Themyscira, earning her eternal gratitude.

TREVOR BARNES

Diana's first real boyfriend was Trevor Barnes, a young man who died heroically while thwarting the evil plans of the Shattered God. Trevor was a former high-school football star who left college to pursue philanthropic work with the Peace Corps. He gained a wealth of experience helping the victims of ethnic wars and abject poverty. He then finished college and joined the staff of the United Nations Rural Development Organization (UNRDO), which helps small poor communities become self-sufficient.

Trevor joined the Peace Corps at age 19 and traveled to Africa and South America, helping with famine relief, agricultural projects, and other charitable work.

FIRST DATE

Diana and Trevor's first date began well, but ended badly. After dinner at a Manhattan bistro, Trevor walked Diana to the Fifth Avenue penthouse apartment she shared with her sister Donna Troy. As they kissed, the visiting hero Tempest accidentally transported them to the savage world of Skartaris!

LOVE IN THE LOST WORLD

Diana and Trevor were hurtled through a portal to Skartaris, an interdimensional realm settled by Atlantean ancestors! Diana saved Trevor from the jaws of a prehistoric sea monster (right), and the two later found themselves thwarting Villainy Inc.'s hostile takeover of Skartaris. Although he was at first overwhelmed by the strangeness in Diana's superheroic life, Trevor adapted quickly and fought bravely to liberate this lost world.

Super-hero Liaisons

RAMA

The avatar of Vishnu, Rama-Chandra met Wonder Woman after Cronus and his progeny ransacked Olympus and attempted to destroy the Hindu gods. The Titan Oblivion trapped Rama and Wonder Woman in a dream realm where the two were united in wedded bliss. The false memories of this illusion were shattered when Diana defeated Oblivion, but Rama's love for her endured.

As the world's most recognized super heroine, Wonder Woman stands among those costumed champions who bridge the gulf between mortal and immortal. Several of these stalwart defenders are her closest friends and allies. Together with the Man of Steel and the Dark Knight, Wonder Woman completes a trinity of the noblest of Earth's super heroes. Aquaman, guardian of the oceans, shares Superman's and Batman's abiding affection for the Amazon Princess, as does Rama, hero of the Hindu pantheon, who also once fought bravely at Wonder Woman's side!

SUPERMAN

Some say that they were destined for each other. He is the world's greatest hero. She is undeniably the world's greatest heroine. Admittedly, there was some attraction between the Man of Steel and the Amazing Amazon, but the two decided they would be better as friends than possible lovers. However, the two found their emotions briefly rekindled while trapped as immortals for a thousand years in Asgard, home of the Norse Gods.

OUR WORLDS AT WAR

Despite rumors to the contrary, Kal-El of Krypton and Diana of Themyscira are just good friends. Each are heroic icons to a troubled world. And both know that for every victory there is also the potential for tragic defeat. The Imperiex War demonstrated to both heroes that they are forever fighting a neverending battle. Circe took advantage of Superman's anger and grief over the fallen victims of that cosmic conflict to transform him into a monster resembling his foe Doomsday. Diana stopped her friend's rampage through New York City, and used her golden lasso to convince him that time heals all wounds.

SPARRING PARTNER
Batman frequently spars with the Amazing Amazon in the JLA's high-tech training facilities. For him it is a chance to learn Amazon martial-arts skills never before mastered by a man. For her it is an opportunity to hone her battle readiness with as daunting a warrior as herself.

DUEL WITH THE DARK KNIGHT

Training with the Dark Knight has brought Diana and Batman's alter ego, Bruce Wayne, closer in friendship. Bruce may even have fallen a little in love with the beautiful heroine. Any lingering affection between the two of them was complicated by Danielle Wellys, a woman accused of murder to whom Wonder Woman gave asylum at the Themysciran Embassy in New York City. Batman's attempts to apprehend Wellys with a G. C. P. D. arrest warrant ended with hero and heroine fighting each other for real!

DON'T. GET. UP.

AQUAMAN

Aquaman, the heroic King of the Seven Seas, is one of Wonder Woman's closest comrades in the ranks of the Justice League. And with good reason. Who better to understand the mind of a monarch than a princess herself? Orin—"Arthur" as he was dubbed by his adoptive human father— and Diana have great respect for each other, and frequently team up together on JLA missions. When Aquaman was missing in action following the Imperiex War, Diana even went so far as to traverse dimensions and inadvertently maroon herself and Trevor Barnes in Skartaris while searching for him.

The couple are quick to play down moments when liking could turn to something more.

WONDER WOMAN'S ENEMIES

DIANA HAS FACED EVIL in all its forms since winning the contest to spread Themyscira's message of peace throughout the world: Ares, God of War, was her first foe, and he has passed on his insatiable appetite for destruction to his own insane progeny of deadly demigods; the demonic Decay and other mythic monsters long to unleash hell on Earth from the depths of Tartarus; the Titan Cronus, father of the Olympian gods who betrayed him, created a child named Devastation to oppose the Amazon Princess; Heracles's hatred for the Amazon sisterhood once ran deep; Circe, enchantress of myth, delights in tormenting Diana with her dark sorcery; the Cheetah would gladly sacrifice the Amazing Amazon to its patron plant-god; Villainy Inc.'s lethal ladies, Doctor Poison and Giganta, assail Wonder Woman with sinister science; Darkseid, ruler of the dreadful world of Apokolips, brought his quest for Anti-Life to Earth from across the cosmos; the Silver Swan, once Diana's young friend, eagerly accepted wicked wings; the wandering spirit Dark Angel sought to drive Diana's mother Hippolyta mad.

And when these fiendish foes have been quelled, there are mortal menaces for Diana to face, such as the Angle Man, the White Magician, Dr. Psycho, and Clayface, each one pursuing his own twisted agenda.

Wonder Woman's Rogues Gallery truly contains the strangest array of adversaries any super hero has ever encountered!

ARES, GOD OF WAR

Ares is master of all weaponry and instruments of war. His ability to manipulate the minds of men sparks conflict and global strife.

HE IS THE AVATAR of aggression, the host of hostility, the epitome of enmity. Since time immemorial, this grim son of Zeus has been mankind's greatest woe. The God of War's desire to conquer and subjugate humanity can be seen in the bitter hatreds and jealousies that have long divided the nations of the Earth. Ares is the original weapon of mass destruction, a god and general, whose battlefield is creation itself. His spoils of war are the souls of every man, woman, and child on the planet. He is Wonder Woman's most implacable foe and, ultimately, he is her reason for existing.

BEFORE THE AMAZONS

IF OLYMPUS TRULY DESIRES TO OWN MEN'S HEARTS— IF POWER IS OUR ULTIMATE AIM— THEN LET ARES DESCEND UPON THESE WEAK-KNEED MORTALS!

In the court of Olympus, Ares beseeched his father Zeus to allow him to descend upon Earth and crush mortal men into eternal submission with his Dogs of War. Although Athena believed that the Olympians themselves might perish if Ares left no one alive to worship them, Zeus turned a blind eye to Ares's scheming.

ALL I NEED DO... IS WAIT!

THE PLOT THICKENS

Artemis, goddess of the Hunt, joined with her Olympian sisters to create a new race of mortals for the glory of Olympus. But Ares had other plans. Even as the Amazons first breathed life, the God of War plotted their ruin. Lies and deceit were his weapons as he pitted mighty Heracles— his stepbrother—against the Amazons. Heracles seduced the Amazon Queen Hippolyta and stole the precious Girdle of Gaea from her. To reclaim it, the peace-loving Amazons went to war against Heracles and his mortal armies. Ares looked on with sadistic glee as the campaign split the sisterhood.

CLASSIC BATTLE

Ares did not destroy the Amazons as he had hoped. However, he succeeded in dividing them into two camps. The one led by Queen Hippolyta reaffirmed devotion to Gaea and to peace; the other, directed by Hippolyta's sister, Antiope, embraced Ares's dark power to ensure its survival. Hippolyta's sisterhood retreated to the island paradise of Themyscira. There they lived in secret for 3,000 years until Hippolyta's yearning for a child was answered by the Olympian goddesses. In Diana, created from Themysciran clay, Hippolyta was given a daughter of peace to thwart Ares's dreams of apocalypse.

"...SHE WOULD DEFEAT THE MADNESS OF THE GOD OF WAR..."

TURNED TO STONE

Wonder Woman was very nearly rid of Ares forever when Cronus, estranged father of Zeus and grandfather of the God of War, destroyed the Hindu gods and usurped their powers to revenge himself upon Olympus. The Olympians were turned to stone, but Diana restored both pantheons to life and joined them in righting the balance of creation. The God of War did not thank Diana for his resurrection. However, he shared the battlefield with his youthful Hindu counterpart to punish the cyclopean centaur Slaughter.

FEEL THE WRATH OF *TWO* WAR GODS!

GODS OF GOTHAM

When crazed crimelord Maxie Zeus and hundreds of religious zealots invoked the darkest forces of Olympus, Gotham City was transformed into a new Tartarus. Soon Ares's terrible children, Eris, Phobos, and Deimos, had possessed the minds and bodies of Batman's arch-foes Poison Ivy, Scarecrow, and the Joker.

To defeat Ares and reclaim Gotham, Wonder Woman joined forces with Wonder Girl, Artemis, and the Bat-Family!

REAL NAME Ares
OCCUPATION God of War
BASE Areopagus, a hill near Olympus
HEIGHT 6 ft 10 in
WEIGHT 359 lb
EYES Red HAIR Unknown
FIRST APPEARANCE
WONDER WOMAN vol. 2 #1
(February 1987)

A church in Gotham City's Hill district was turned into a hideous temple dedicated to Ares.

CHILDREN OF ARES

THE WAR GOD'S CHILDREN share their brutal father's unending hatred for Wonder Woman. Dedicated to destruction, nearly all of Ares's offspring have aided and abetted his cruel campaigns to sow the seeds of devastating wars and so bring about mankind's downfall. Phobos, the God of Fear, is able to make his foes' worst nightmares physically real. Deimos is the God of Terror, and his beard of serpents bites with panic-inducing venom. Eris is the Goddess of Strife and the possessor of the Golden Apples of Discord, which bring only rancor and hatred to anyone foolish enough to taste their bitter fruit!

HARMONIA

Ares's other daughter was Harmonia, Goddess of Balance. She supported peace, but the thread of her destiny was cut tragically short. The Fates warned her of the War of the Gods that would threaten Earth, and Harmonia helped Wonder Woman during the conflict but was slain by her brother Phobos. However, she left Diana her powerful amulet. With it, Diana had her own secret gateway to Ares's base in Tartarus and the netherworld.

QUEZALCOATL

Circe sparked the War of the Gods hoping that the war deities of many pantheons would wipe one another out. Ares and his children, Phobos and Eris, were vital to Circe's plans. To distract Superman from interfering in his forays on Earth, Phobos awoke the winged serpent Quezalcoatl, the Aztec god of wind, clouds, and rain. After a brief battle in the skies above the South American jungle, Superman realized Quezalcoatl was not evil, but had the welfare of the rainforest and its peoples at heart.

THE APPLES OF DISCORD

Eris lives in mythic infamy as the goddess who started the epic Trojan War. In modern times, Eris used her magic apples to disrupt the Themysciran summit which brought representatives of Patriarch's World to the Amazons' island paradise for reconciliation and unity. However, reporter Lois Lane was on hand to recount Wonder Woman's escape from Eris's Tree of Discord and help to defeat the goddess of strife!

DEIMOS DECAPITATED!

When Ares and his sons threatened to start a nuclear war, Wonder Woman used Harmonia's amulet to breach the evil gods' netherworld base! There, Diana and a small army of her closest friends engaged Deimos and Phobos. Deimos entangled Diana with his venomous serpents. Diana fought off the fear-inducing venom and beheaded Deimos with her razor-sharp tiara!

GODS OF GOTHAM

Following their crushing defeat, the children of Ares swore in their father's name to never again interfere in the affairs of man. However, Phobos, Deimos (miraculously resurrected), and Eris schemed a way to get around the pact while still being true to their vows. By inhabiting the bodies of Batman's arch-foes—Joker, Scarecrow, and Poison Ivy respectively—the children of Ares were able to infiltrate Gotham City without ever physically setting foot on Earth. Empowered by the psychic energies of a band of religious zealots led by deranged former crime boss Maxie Zeus, the war god's spawn transformed Gotham into a new base from which their father could carry on his relentless war upon mankind!

REBELLIOUS CHILDREN

At the height of battle, Phobos took over Batman's body and became the ultimate God of Fear! Mad with their augmented powers, the children of Ares renounced their father. Wonder Woman convinced Ares of his brood's betrayal. And together, the God of War and Wonder Woman defeated the upstart Gods of Gotham.

ARES'S PUNISHMENT

With a wave of his hand, Ares separated his children from their Bat-Rogue forms and all three were sent straight to Hades. Phobos received the worst punishment – chained to Ixion's wheel in the underworld.

HERACLES

IN THE ANNALS OF GREEK MYTHOLOGY, Heracles is remembered as a hero and helper to both the gods and mankind. Yet Heracles was a flawed figure, driven as much by the strength of his passions as his celebrated strength. Son of Zeus and the mortal Alcmene, Heracles's name translates as "Hera's Glory," a bitter irony considering that the goddess and wife of Zeus persecuted Heracles throughout his mortal life. Heracles is perhaps best known in myth for the Twelve Labors he had to perform for slaying his own wife and sons. However, to the Amazon sisterhood, his name will forever live in infamy as the man who brutally betrayed their trust and tried to enslave them.

FALLING FROM GRACE
Under the influence of Ares, Heracles led his stepbrother Theseus and their warriors to march upon the city-state of Themyscira, home to the Amazons. On the plains beyond the city's gates, Heracles faced the Amazon Queen Hippolyta, who showed the demigod that his brute strength was no match for her superior combat skills.

TRUCE AND TREACHERY
Soundly defeated, Heracles surrendered with a hearty laugh and called a truce. However, that night, while the Amazons cordially traded food, wine, and song with Heracles's men, the son of Zeus was busy hatching other plans!

HERACLES STRIKES!
Lulled by the promise of peace and attracted by Heracles's rugged charm and mighty physique, the Amazon Queen accepted a drugged cup of mead. The potion weakened Hippolyta, and Heracles easily overpowered her.

REAL NAME Heracles
OCCUPATION God
BASE Olympus
HEIGHT 6 ft 4 in
WEIGHT 220 lb
EYES Brown HAIR Brown
FIRST APPEARANCE
WONDER WOMAN vol. 2 #1
(February 1987)

HIPPOLYTA CHAINED
Heracles chained Hippolyta in a dungeon while his men ransacked Themyscira, killing, ravaging, and pillaging without mercy. Heracles utterly humiliated Hippolyta, stripping from her the prized Girdle of Gaea as a symbol of his conquest over the Amazons.

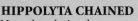

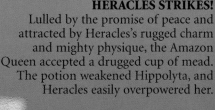

THE PUNISHMENT OF HERACLES

Heracles should have known that the gods—and his own father Zeus chief among them—would be enraged by the evils inflicted upon the Amazons. After all, the Olympians had created the Amazons to lead mankind in the ways of peace. Furious, Zeus sentenced Heracles to support the weight of the Amazons' new island home upon his mighty shoulders for nearly 3,000 years.

THE RETURN
At last Wonder Woman freed Heracles from his burden and he became the first man to set foot on the Amazons' island paradise. Humbled by his centuries of punishment, he begged the sisterhood for forgiveness. The Amazons gracefully accepted his sincere repentance. Having finally shown himself to be a true man, Heracles ascended as a god to Mount Olympus.

THE GREAT PRETENDER

Soon after taking his place among the Olympians, Heracles returned to Earth. This time he came in the guise of billionaire recluse Harold Campion, otherwise known as the super-strong Champion, Gateway City's newest super hero. Wonder Woman had no idea that the brash and arrogant Champion had once been the bane of all Amazons. In reality, Heracles was playing out a secret plan that began with a stolen kiss from Diana and a potion not unlike the one that had led to Hippolyta's humiliation. To preserve his deception, Champion aided Wonder Woman on several adventures. Meanwhile, Heracles plotted against the Amazing Amazon.

UNMASKED AND REJECTED
Despite past protestations, Heracles still burned with resentment. "Champion" was just a scheme to seduce Diana and turn her against the Amazons. Champion's identity was revealed by the priestess Eudia as Diana and her sisters were turned into clay! Heracles beseeched the gods to restore Diana and the Amazons to life. He also confessed that he had lost his heart to Wonder Woman. But Diana did not return Heracles's love—and that was perhaps punishment enough for his sins.

CIRCE

THE EVIL ENCHANTRESS Circe has the power to bring out the beast in man! She acquired her powers after making a pact with the witch-goddess Hecate. She can teleport, create complex illusions, and transform herself to resemble anyone or anything she wishes. But ever since discovering Wonder Woman's existence, she has channeled all her energies into sinister schemes against the Amazons of Themyscira. In battle with Wonder Woman, Circe frequently alters her appearance to keep Diana off-guard.

THE ISLE OF AEAEA

For untold centuries, this siren sorceress lured sailors to their deaths off the cursed shores of Aeaea. Those unlucky survivors spared a quick death at sea found themselves transformed into the bizarre "Bestiamorph" abominations—every one her slave—that populated Circe's island home.

REAL NAME Circe
OCCUPATION Sorceress
BASE Formerly Aeaea; now mobile
HEIGHT 5 ft 9 in
WEIGHT 125 lb
EYES Red HAIR Violet
FIRST APPEARANCE
WONDER WOMAN vol. 2 #17
(June 1988)

WILD THINGS

Long ago, Circe discovered alien remains in what is now the Middle Eastern nation of Qurac. This dead extraterrestrial flesh became the main ingredient in her Bestiamorph potion, capable of turning men into beasts.

BITING THE BIG APPLE

One of Circe's most ambitious attacks was aimed not at Diana, but at the President of the United States, Lex Luthor. Circe transformed the entire male population of New York City into Bestiamorphs. She then loosed a posse of femme fatales to hunt them! Wonder Woman assembled a squadron of super-heroines and descended on the streets of Manhattan. But Circe had one more trick up her sleeve: she turned Superman into a Super-Bestiamorph (far right), mixing Superman's powers with the animal angst of the Kryptonian creature Doomsday!

LYTA'S LOVE

Circe escaped capture in New York City. But Wonder Woman caught up with the wicked witch in the ruins of the Parthenon in Greece. It might have been their final battle if not for Circe's young daughter, Lyta.

CIRCE'S DAUGHTER

The child Hippolyta is the result of Circe's brief dalliance with the war god Ares while she lived under the guise of attorney Donna Milton, and he dominated Boston's criminal underworld as the mortal Ares Buchanan. Circe named their daughter Hippolyta ("Lyta" for short), although her reasons for doing so are unknown. It remains to be seen how much of her parents' supernatural might Lyta has inherited.

VENGEANCE AND MERCY

On the steps of the Parthenon, close to the place where Diana's mother Hippolyta died, Circe taunted Wonder Woman to kill her as the world looked on. But Diana refused to give in to hate. Instead of a clenched fist, Wonder Woman offered her greatest female foe the hand of compassion and mercy.

CHEETAH I

BARBARA ANN MINERVA was always more of a treasure hunter than a traditional archaeologist. Rather than preserving antiquities, Minerva sought historical artifacts that would further her own fame and fortune. On one expedition, Minerva trekked through the jungles of Africa and discovered the lost temple that was home to the plant-god Urzkartaga. Enticed by the promise of great power, Minerva embraced the secrets of Urzkartaga. She endured a bloodletting ritual that transformed her into a vessel for the Cheetah, a feral fiend driven to hunt down human prey!

As the Cheetah, Minerva possessed superhuman strength, speed, and agility.

Razor-sharp claws capable of rending flesh and scoring stone.

URZKARTAGA
The god Urzkartaga demanded human sacrifice. A Sudanese tribe of zealots abducted victims from neighboring tribes to supply fresh blood for the ceremony that revived Urzkartaga's protector, the Cheetah.

THE PRIEST CHUMA
When Barbara Minerva's expedition discovered the temple, the Urzkartagans killed all but Minerva and her partner, Dr. Leavens, who escaped together into the jungle. After witnessing another tribe attack the Urzkartagans during their bloodletting ritual, Minerva forced the Urzkartagan priest Chuma to reveal the secrets of the ritual. He did so, and Minerva killed Leavens to offer his blood to Urzkartaga. Minerva became the Cheetah and Chuma stayed by her, helping to renew her powers while he tended the plant-god.

REAL NAME Barbara Ann Minerva
OCCUPATION Archaeologist
BASE Nottingham, England
HEIGHT 5 ft 9 in
WEIGHT 120 lb
EYES Brown HAIR Auburn
FIRST APPEARANCE
WONDER WOMAN vol. 2 #7
(August 1987)

BLOOD RITUAL

A magical elixir held the secret to the Cheetah's power, and only Chuma knew how to make it. He fed fresh blood to the plant-god, mashed the plant's berries into a paste and made a potion. He painted Minerva's face and she drank the brew. Her body writhed as the power of the Cheetah possessed her!

FELINE FATALE
When Chuma was killed, Minerva sold her soul to the demon Neron and became even more powerful in order to resurrect her faithful servant.

THE WHITE MAGICIAN'S PET
An unholy ceremony turned The White Magician into a Lord High Daemon. To retain his terrible power he sacrificed his "pet," Cheetah, and his hapless girlfriend, Cassie Arnold.

FERAL ATTRACTION

As the Cheetah, Barbara Minerva discovered the lost city of the Bana-Mighdall and slaughtered many Amazons before Diana stopped her. Circe later freed Minerva from Gotham City's Arkham Asylum and forced her to drink a potion that made the Cheetah the sorceress's slave. In Boston, the Cheetah became an assassin for mobster Paulie Longo. Minerva briefly reformed and became Wonder Woman's friend before the White Magician turned her into a demon. After selling her soul to Neron, Minerva lost control of her Cheetah persona and cut a bloody swath through Gateway City before Diana helped Minerva exorcize the plant-god in a psychic ritual.

CHEETAH II

CORPORATE RAIDER Sébastian Ballesteros clawed his way up from the depths of poverty to become one of the most powerful men in Argentina. Raised in a Buenos Aires shantytown, young Sébastian lost his only brother in a military coup. Later, his parents vanished, like countless others during the military government's "societal cleansing." Sébastian, however, embraced the dictators and used their influence to become wealthy. But that wasn't enough for him. Sébastian knew that power always trumped riches. And to achieve such power, he was willing to embrace Urzkartaga and become the new Cheetah!

THEY DEMAND THE POWER OF URZKARTAGA!

TRANSFORMATION

Sébastian Ballesteros despised his humble beginnings and vowed to do anything to rise above them. When he learned of the awesome power of Urzkartaga, he entered into negotiations like a true scheming businessman and offered the plant-god an offer it couldn't refuse.

Retractable, razor-sharp claws.

Strong prehensile tail.

URZKARTAGA

No one knows how Sébastian Ballesteros discovered the secrets of Urzkartaga, or how he came to possess the plant god itself, which resided in Sébastian's private sanctum in the Ballesteros Building. With his bargaining savvy, Ballesteros convinced Urzkartaga to abandon its female host, Barbara Minerva, and allow a male to once more be the conduit for the ancient powers of the Cheetah!

CHEETAH POWER

Ballesteros's Cheetah possesses super-strength and can strike at amazing speed. His fearsome claws and teeth can rend metal. He possesses a prehensile tail and hyper-acute senses to stalk with feline stealth and slay any victim !

REAL NAME Sébastian Ballesteros
OCCUPATION Industrialist
BASE Buenos Aires, Argentina
HEIGHT 6 ft (6 ft 10 in as Cheetah)
WEIGHT 185 lb EYES Brown
HAIR Black with graying temples
FIRST APPEARANCE
WONDER WOMAN #143
(April 1999)

Manly mane.

BALLESTEROS' H.Q.
The banking and financial transactions carried out in the Ballesteros Building are just fronts for Sébastian's dabblings in other, less orthodox businesses, including mystical mergers and the manufacture of bio-weapons like the second Silver Swan!

WAITING TO POUNCE
Wonder Woman was caught unawares when first attacked by Ballesteros. Preoccupied by Vanessa Kapatelis's rampage through New York City as the Silver Swan, Diana walked right into an ambush by the all-new—and even more ferocious—Cheetah.

BUT-- BUT YOU'RE A MAN!

ALL IN THE FAMILY
To further his climb to power, Ballesteros made a pact with Circe to turn Diana's friend, Vanessa Kapatelis, into a second Silver Swan. He also became Circe's lover as she sought to assemble her own warped family to wage war upon Wonder Woman!

THE UNKINDEST CAT OF ALL!
Barbara Minerva didn't take kindly to Sébastian Ballesteros's hostile takeover of the Cheetah. To reclaim her stolen powers she turned to an even darker spirit, the "Kindly One" Tisiphone!

THE SPIRIT OF VENGEANCE
Minerva plotted to seize back the powers of the Cheetah by allowing Tisiphone, the Greek spirit of vengeance, to possess her. Her own anger further inflamed by Tisiphone's unending rage, Minerva hunted Ballesteros down. The two fought to a standstill until they were nearly crushed by a collapsing building. Minerva apparently died, while Ballesteros remained the Cheetah. But for how long remains to be seen.

VILLAINY INC.

TWO DIFFERENT GENERATIONS have known the threat of Villainy Incorporated. And two different Wonder Women have battled this fiendish formation of femme fatales. Queen Hippolyta first fought Villainy Inc. during World War II, when the evil Clea, deposed Queen of Venturia, assembled the very first Cheetah, Doctor Poison, Hypnotic Woman, and the sorceress Zara to attack Atlantis! Villainy Inc. failed then, but Clea's determination was undying. Decades later, the villainess gathered together a new Villainy Inc. for a fresh assault.

RIOT GIRLS

Clea's second incarnation of Villainy Inc. included the cybernetic siren Cyborgirl, the original Doctor Poison's ghastly granddaughter, the giantess Giganta, East Indian sorceress Jinx, and the mysterious Trinity, whose three terrible faces concealed her insidious intentions!

Giganta

Jinx

Cyborgirl

Clea

Trinity

Doctor Poison

UNDER SIEGE

Clea was unaware that Atlantis had been transported to another dimension during the Imperiex War. While searching for it, Clea found the gateway to the savage realm of Skartaris. Soon Clea and the new Villainy Inc. had invaded Skartaris and marched on its fabled city, Shamballah.

...AND *REBOOT* THE CORE AND *RESET* THE CONTINENT...

...BY *REWINDING* TIME.

IN THE SAVAGE WORLD OF SKARTARIS LIFE IS A CONSTANT STRUGGLE FOR SURVIVAL.

THE TRINITY VIRUS

However a traitor existed within Villainy Inc.'s ranks— Trinity! While Cyborgirl accessed a super-computer located beneath Shamballah, Trinity revealed her true self! She was a living computer virus designed to infect the Shamballah mainframe and reestablish the glory of old Atlantis by turning back the clock! Diana eradicated the Trinity Virus, but many parts of Skartaris suffered from Trinity's destructive effects.

BAKWELE KIRUS, THE SLAVE CITY OF BAL SHAZAR KALTBAS, CITADEL OF TINGAD, THE TEMPLE OF SUN...

ALL OUTPOSTS, ALL CITY SYSTEMS ARE UNDER OUR COMMAND.

TRINITY

Before becoming a member of Villainy Inc., Trinity battled the Teen Titans with her three vile visages. The Face of War fires force-bolts; the Face of Chaos assaults the minds of her victims; and the Face of Time speeds up, slows down, or even stops time itself.

CYBORGIRL

LeTonya Charles destroyed her body with the drug known as "Tar," but LeTonya's aunt Sarah Charles saved her niece from death with powerful cybernetic implants. These replaced much of LeTonya's humanity with hardware. Perhaps this is why LeTonya has yet to use her new lease on life for anything other than personal gain.

CLEA

As Queen of Venturia, a crumbling Atlantean outpost, Clea enslaved the men of her realm and amused herself by putting many to death in gladiatorial combat. But what she really wanted was Aurania, Venturia's flourishing sister city and the first step towards dominion over the entire lost continent of Atlantis! Clea stole the fabled trident of Poseidon to make herself virtually unstoppable!

JINX

Little is known of the witch Jinx. She wields emerald fire and can transmute elements, create devastating tremblers, or launch lightning bolts from her hands, but only while her bare feet touch the Earth. Jinx once fought Donna Troy and her fellow Titans as a member of the Fearsome Five.

DR. POISON

A TOXIC AVENGER, the diabolical Doctor Poison carries on a legacy begun by her grandmother, the Imperial Japanese spy Princess Maru. During World War II, Maru used her sinister scientific savvy as both an Axis agent and as a member of the original Villainy Inc. Both associations brought Doctor Poison into conflict with Queen Hippolyta in her guise as wartime Wonder Woman. Decades later, Maru's granddaughter took up the role of Doctor Poison with a venomous vengeance. She allied herself with one of Wonder Woman's newest nemeses in order to unleash the terrible Pandora Virus upon the world!

POISONOUS BREATH

Dr. Poison's self-experimentation has made her body a host for banes and blights of every sort. Like other venomous creatures, Dr. Poison herself is immune to the poisons she breathes out or exudes from her skin.

BAD MEDICINE

Dr. Poison presents a deliberately ghoulish face to the world. Molecularly bonded appliqués peel back her eyelids to achieve a permanent stare. Dental hooks pull her lips into a rictus of revulsion. A drying agent fed from her costume to her salivary glands keeps her mouth from drooling excessively.

REAL NAME Unrevealed
OCCUPATION Scientist
BASE Mobile
HEIGHT 5 ft 4 in
WEIGHT 119 lb
EYES Gray HAIR Black
FIRST APPEARANCE
WONDER WOMAN vol. 2 #151
(December 1999)

REVERSO OF FORTUNE

The original Dr. Poison perished when she fell victim to her own "Reverso" toxin. This regressed her in age from adult to child to fetus and beyond, until she disappeared!

UNDER THE KNIFE
No one knows whether Dr. Poison realizes that the Wonder Woman she has encountered is the same heroine who thwarted her ancestor during World War II. But upon meeting the Amazing Amazon, the new Dr. Poison was very eager to subject Diana to a few experiments—all in the cause of science, of course!

HORROR TRIAL
Dr. Poison's most sadistic scheme to date has been the creation of the so-called "Pandora Virus." Using a very secret ingredient, Dr. Poison engineered a potential plague that freed the myths of the subconscious mind and made them horrifyingly real!

POISON IN THE AIR
The first person to be infected by the Pandora Virus was Richard Thomas Agoras, an unwilling participant in Dr. Poison's trials. Although he was released with no memory of the experiments he endured, Agoras later mutated into a giant spider! Wonder Woman, aided by the blue-skinned warrior Rama, freed Agoras from the grip of the Pandora Virus, but was unable to stop Dr. Poison from releasing the contagion as an airborne plague!

THE LIVING DEAD
Like her grandmother, the new Dr. Poison also joined Queen Clea's Villainy Inc. As this gang sought to conquer the other-dimensional land of Skartaris, Dr. Poison donated her "Body Banks" to the cause, reanimating dead victims with her chemical concoctions into super-strong zombie soldiers!

BLOOD OF DEVASTATION
Unknown to Wonder Woman, the true source of the Pandora Virus was the demon-child Devastation, one of the Titan Cronus's monstrous offspring. She donated her own lifeblood —seething with all her father's evil and bitterness—to unleash the worst nightmares of the soul upon every man, woman, and child on Earth!

GIGANTA

FROM STRICKEN SCIENTIST to rampaging gorilla and size-altering giantess, Dr. Doris Zeul has lived many lives. And each time she has been Wonder Woman's adversary. Terminally ill, Dr. Zeul was determined to preserve her brilliant brain. She longed to possess Wonder Woman's perfect physique, but was forced to pick less ideal donors. Dr. Zeul now occupies the giant form of Giganta, but she still hopes to separate Diana's mind from her body and replace it with her own!

DR. DORIS ZEUL
After developing a fatal blood disease, Dr. Zeul devoted her remaining days to devising a means of saving her consciousness. Success came when Zeul invented a method of transferring one creature's mind into another's body.

THE BODY-SNATCHER
When Wonder Woman was struck down by the demon lord Neron, Dr. Zeul saw her opportunity and stole Diana's body. However, before Dr. Zeul could transfer her own mind into Diana's helpless form, Hippolyta and Cassie Sandsmark intervened!

WONDER GIRL VS. GORILLA WOMAN
Because Hippolyta halted Zeul's process in mid-transference, the dying scientist's consciousness was drawn into a "buffer module" of her mind-swapping apparatus. There Zeul languished in limbo until her loyal lab assistant freed Zeul's mind by transferring it into the body of Giganta, a gorilla test subject. The simian switcheroo complete, Giganta killed Zeul's lab assistant and grappled with Wonder Girl before escaping!

WAKE UP, MY DARLING, WE'RE GOING TO GET YOU HELP. JUST OPEN YOUR EYES...

IT WAS THAT DAMN SHAMAN. HE CAST SOME SORT OF SPELL ON OLGA. QUICKLY, GET AN AMBULANCE. GET HELP!

TAEEEE

MIND TRANSFER

Through circumstances not yet fully revealed, Zeul—as the gorilla Giganta—kidnapped a strongwoman named Olga from the Balthazar Circus. Later, Zeul transferred her mind into Olga's body, but retained the moniker "Giganta" as her alter ego in the criminal gang Villainy Inc.

REAL NAME Dr. Doris Zeul

OCCUPATION
Scientist/strongwoman

BASE Mobile

HEIGHT 6 ft 6 in WEIGHT 220 lb

EYES Green HAIR Red

FIRST APPEARANCE
WONDER WOMAN vol. 2 #125
(September 1997)

ABILITY TO CHANGE SIZE

The sorceress Clea may be responsible for Giganta's newly-acquired ability to change size, growing from human proportions to hundreds of feet tall in seconds, and gaining hugely in strength!

AGGH!

TBA SLAMM

BOOM

BOOM

THE BIGGER THEY ARE, THE HARDER THEY FALL!

Giganta took part in Villainy Inc.'s attempted takeover of other-dimensional Skartaris. She led a gaggle of gargantuan gladiators into guerilla combat with Wonder Woman's liberating forces. But even at plus-size, Giganta was no match for Diana's powerful punch!

12

SILVER SWAN

OF ALL DIANA'S ADVERSARIES, the Silver Swan's story is perhaps the most tragic. It is a study in carefully calculated, man-made evil that begins with the deformed and deranged figure of Valerie Beaudry and ends with the mentally manipulated Vanessa Kapatelis. In both cases, utterly ruthless industrialists were to blame. Nuclear mutation and a desperate desire for love transformed fragile Valerie Beaudry into the first Silver Swan. Years later, the gruesome process was repeated to turn college student Vanessa Kapetelis, one of Wonder Woman's closest friends, into a freakish, winged weapon!

SILVER SWAN I

Her parents' exposure to radiation from nuclear tests resulted in Valerie Beaudry being born horribly deformed. Valerie had no friends except for a pen pal named Henry Cobb Armbruster. The head of Armbruster International, he exploited Valerie's need for acceptance by choosing her for his Silver Swan project, turning her into a siren with deadly superpowers. He married her, then sent his Silver Swan swooping after Wonder Woman!

THE SWAN'S SONG

Armbruster's experiments gave Valerie wings and the power to amplify her voice to create a protective shield or an ear-splitting, destructive scream!

SEBASTIAN BALLESTEROS
Using the old Armbruster International files, insidious industrialist Ballesteros duplicated the original Silver Swan experiments.

SILVER SWAN II

Sébastian Ballesteros abducted Diana's young friend Vanessa Kapatelis and used the telepathic traumas inflicted upon her by Dr. Psycho to turn Vanessa into a revenging raptor! Like her predecessor, this new Silver Swan can fly. Cybernetic surgery to her vocal chords has given Vanessa a screeching sonic scream, and psionic enhancement allows her to control birds with her mind. In addition, Vanessa's eyes have been altered to give her the sharp vision of a bird of prey.

WALL OF SOUND
More powerful than the first Silver Swan, Vanessa's "swan song" can unleash a scream with the force of a hurricane, capable of smashing concrete to rubble!

SKREEEEE

BAWOOOM

REAL NAME Vanessa Kapatelis
OCCUPATION Winged weapon
BASE Boston
HEIGHT 5 ft 6 in WEIGHT 125 lb
EYES Silver (formerly blue)
HAIR Red (naturally brown)
FIRST APPEARANCE
WONDER WOMAN vol. 2 #3
(April 1987)

BIRDS OF A FEATHER...
...attack together, as the new Silver Swan demonstrated when she flew to Gateway City accompanied by an army of birds whipped into a frenzy of sharp talons and gnashing beaks! Insanely jealous of Diana's close friends Helena and Cassie Sandsmark, the Silver Swan destroyed the Gateway City Museum in a vain attempt to kill curator Helena. Afterwards, she flew off to attack Cassie at her high school!

BAD FEELING
Vanessa burned with hatred towards Cassie Sandsmark for becoming Wonder Girl, believing that the role of Wonder Woman's youthful ally should have been hers!

AN EVIL INFLUENCE
Diana learned that the sorceress Circe was ultimately responsible for Vanessa's transformation into the Silver Swan. High above the streets of New York City, Wonder Woman begged Vanessa to turn away from her new mistress. In the tumult, the Silver Swan escaped. For both their sakes, Wonder Woman hopes that her next encounter with Vanessa will be as friends once more.

CRONUS

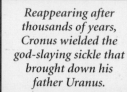

BEFORE OLYMPUS and its pantheon there was Cronus. Born to Gaea the Earth and Uranus the Sky, Cronus was the first of the twelve Titans who would sire the Olympian gods and goddesses. But before he could rule creation, Cronus had to murder his own father. Later, a prophecy revealed that Cronus would suffer the same fate at the hands of his own son, Zeus. So Cronus lay dormant until he could take his revenge upon his Olympian children and also on Wonder Woman!

Reappearing after thousands of years, Cronus wielded the god-slaying sickle that brought down his father Uranus.

REAL NAME Cronus
OCCUPATION Titan
BASE The Universe
HEIGHT 10 ft
WEIGHT 360 lb
EYES Red   HAIR White
FIRST APPEARANCE
THE NEW TITANS #51
(Winter 1988)

Within Cronus's corpse was his sons' agreement to divide creation among themselves. Zeus would rule the heavens; Poseidon the seas; and Hades the underworld.

SLAYING THE SKY

Where Cronus and his fellow Titans were visions of divine beauty, their siblings the Cyclops were vile monsters in the eyes of Uranus, who cast them into the bowels of Tartarus. Gaea could not forgive Uranus for exiling her children to that deep, dark pit, and gave her most devoted son Cronus the sickle with which he killed his father!

BAND OF BROTHERS

As Cronus killed his own father, so it was fated that the son of Cronus would murder *him*. Cronus tried to prevent this by consuming his own children as soon as his wife Rhea gave birth to them. But Rhea hid the infant Zeus from her husband. In manhood, Zeus sent his wife Metis to seduce Cronus and force him to vomit up his sons Hades and Poseidon. Reunited with his brothers, Zeus plotted his father's downfall as destiny foretold!

SHOT THROUGH THE HEART

In a titanic battle, the brother gods slayed Cronus. Zeus pierced his heart with a magic arrow.

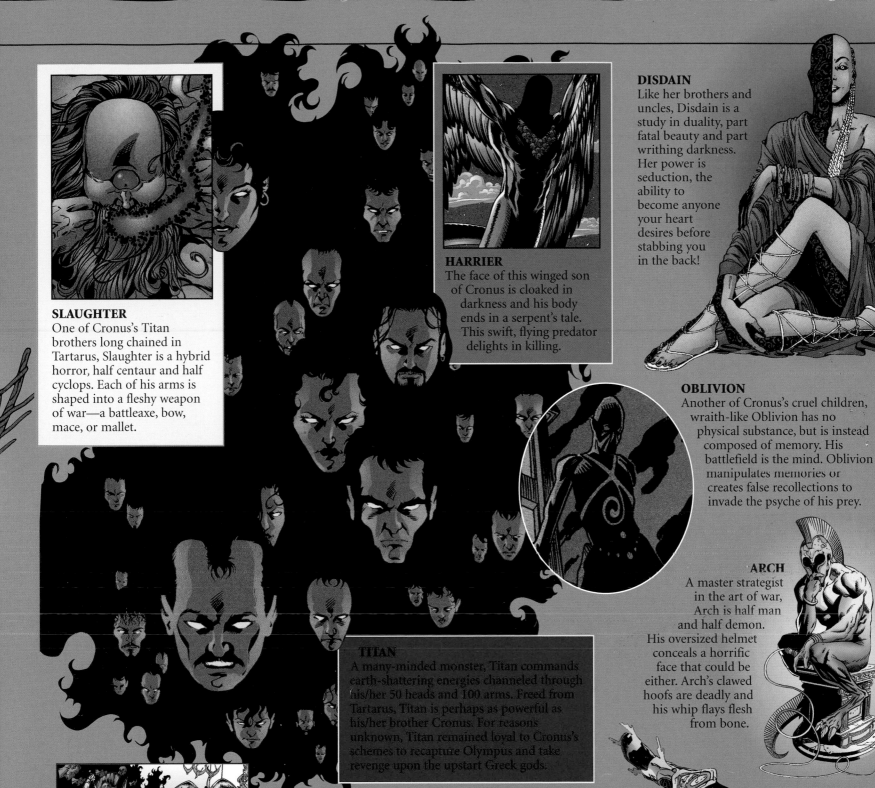

SLAUGHTER

One of Cronus's Titan brothers long chained in Tartarus, Slaughter is a hybrid horror, half centaur and half cyclops. Each of his arms is shaped into a fleshy weapon of war—a battleaxe, bow, mace, or mallet.

HARRIER

The face of this winged son of Cronus is cloaked in darkness and his body ends in a serpent's tale. This swift, flying predator delights in killing.

DISDAIN

Like her brothers and uncles, Disdain is a study in duality, part fatal beauty and part writhing darkness. Her power is seduction, the ability to become anyone your heart desires before stabbing you in the back!

OBLIVION

Another of Cronus's cruel children, wraith-like Oblivion has no physical substance, but is instead composed of memory. His battlefield is the mind. Oblivion manipulates memories or creates false recollections to invade the psyche of his prey.

ARCH

A master strategist in the art of war, Arch is half man and half demon. His oversized helmet conceals a horrific face that could be either. Arch's clawed hoofs are deadly and his whip flays flesh from bone.

TITAN

A many-minded monster, Titan commands earth-shattering energies channeled through his/her 50 heads and 100 arms. Freed from Tartarus, Titan is perhaps as powerful as his/her brother Cronus. For reasons unknown, Titan remained loyal to Cronus's schemes to recapture Olympus and take revenge upon the upstart Greek gods.

CLASH OF THE TITANS

Eventually, Cronus was magically brought back to life. He freed Titan and Slaughter from Tartarus and plotted to regain his omnipotence. With an army of gods at his command, he turned the Hindu and Olympian pantheons to stone and stole their divine powers. Thus armed, he turned his campaign towards Heaven itself in a bid to claim the Presence, the force of creation. But as Cronus and his children clashed with Heaven's angels, Wonder Woman freed the Hindu and Olympian gods and led the final assault against the father of all gods!

THE END OF CRONUS

Diana shattered the sickle that was the source of Cronus's might, and he returned to the arms of his mother Gaea.

DEVASTATION

THIS BABY-FACED CHILD, barely 12 years old, is one of Wonder Woman's most cunning and alarming foes. For Devastation is the monstrous, shape-changing offspring of the utterly evil Titan Cronus, sworn enemy of the Gods of Olympus. Cronus fashioned her from the very same clay from which Wonder Woman was first formed. His purpose was to create a being that would answer Wonder Woman's bright challenge to his dark powers, a creature that would spread despair and chaos on Earth.

PROMISE OF DOOM

Cronus vowed that his latest child, Devastation, would become central to the future history of the world. All of his other monstrous children—Harrier, Disdain, Titan, Slaughter, Arch, and Oblivion—gathered round to bestow their blessings.

I, CRONUS, GIVE HER THE GIFT OF LIFE, AND THE NAME THAT SHALL SUNDER THE WORLD... DEVASTATION!

THE FIRST MEETING

Wonder Woman first encountered Devastation when the child of evil had taken on the name Deva and the form of a super-cool teenager. While a normally peaceful town erupted in senseless violence, the two fought for supremacy. Devastation proved Wonder Woman's match in combat, and Diana was fortunate to escape with her life.

DO YOU NOW! LET ME GIVE YOU SOME ANSWERS, WONDERING WOMAN

CAUSING CHAOS

Devastation's aim is, little by little, to subvert Wonder Woman's benign influence over the hearts and minds of ordinary Americans, and turn people into unstable, merciless missionaries of discord, prejudice, and brutality. Once brainwashed by Devastation's mind control, these poor, misguided souls spread chaos and misery wherever they go. Only Wonder Woman can spoil Devastation's fun.

DEADLY FOE

With mindless violence flaring up everywhere, Wonder Woman was forced to fly hither and thither saving lives and restoring peace. "You might as well try to save an ant-hill one ant at a time," mocked Devastation. Yet Diana remained true to her purpose, knowing that every human life was precious. But how could she convince Devastation to spare humanity?

VICIOUS ATTACK
Despite her tender years, Devastation has amazing strength. When, as Deva, she was first challenged by Wonder Woman, she caught the Amazon Princess off guard and sent her flying. After nearly knocking Wonder Woman unconscious, she weakened her with a gunshot wound.

THE TRUTH HURTS
Wonder Woman finally managed to overpower Deva and entangle her in her golden Lasso of Truth. The deadly teen immediately reverted to her true shape as the child-like Devastation. But a further shock was in store for Wonder Woman: Devastation was able to use the Lasso to discover all of Wonder Woman's strengths and weaknesses, and there was nothing Diana could do about it!

REAL NAME Devastation
OCCUPATION Creator of mayhem
BASE Earth
HEIGHT 4 ft 6 in
WEIGHT 82 lb
EYES Pale blue   HAIR Red
FIRST APPEARANCE
WONDER WOMAN vol. 2 #143
(April 1999)

DISASTER AVERTED
The climax of Devastation's scheme to spread chaos throughout the world involved manipulating a terrorist group to explode a nuclear bomb. However, Devastation was unaware that Wonder Woman had mixed a drop of her own blood in the clay from which Devastation had been created. Diana successfully appealed to this drop of goodness in the evil child and the bomb exploded harmlessly underground.

DARK ANGEL

THE BRINGER OF DOOM known as "Dark Angel" has long bedeviled humans foolish enough to summon her. During World War II, Nazi occult mistress Paula Von Gunther called forth this wandering evil spirit, who then took over Von Gunther's body and attacked Wonder Woman and the Justice Society of America with her mystical might. The JSA ultimately triumphed, but Dark Angel would henceforth regard Hippolyta as her number one enemy. While attempting to kidnap Hippolyta's daughter Diana, Dark Angel mistakenly abducted Diana's magically created "twin," Donna, who would suffer many lifetimes of torment as part of Dark Angel's scheme to drive Hippolyta insane!

WHO'S GONNA STOP ME?

A LIVING HELL
Dark Angel forced Diana's "twin" to live many tortured lives, including life as a woman with a cruel and abusive husband.

WHO IS DONNA TROY?
Little by little, Diana's "twin" was strengthened by Dark Angel's multiple manipulations of reality. The twin became "Donna Troy," a distinct individual who would one day rejoin Diana and Hippolyta.

HITLER'S HELPER

By capturing the mystical Bahdnesian Thunderbolt belonging to the Justice Society's Johnny Thunder, Paula Von Gunther thought she possessed the power to help the Third Reich's drive for world conquest. Von Gunther intended to be the focus of that power herself, but accidentally summoned Dark Angel instead! The evil spirit possessed Von Gunther. And since Von Gunther was loyal to Nazi Germany's tyrant leader Adolf Hitler, Dark Angel was also obliged to grant Hitler his fondest wish: the destruction of the JSA!

REAL NAME Unknown
OCCUPATION Wandering Spirit
BASE Mobile
HEIGHT 6 ft 10 in
WEIGHT 185 lb
EYES Red HAIR Black
FIRST APPEARANCE
WONDER WOMAN vol. 2 #131
(March 1998)

THUNDERSTRUCK

Paula Von Gunther may have caught Johnny Thunder's Thunderbolt, but Dark Angel knew just how to keep the pink genie bottled up inside Von Gunther's crystal magic wand. Forced to do Dark Angel's bidding, the Thunderbolt lured the JSA into a trap.

NO...NO MORE! NO MORE! JUST TELL ME WHAT YOU WANT!!

ANGEL OF DEATH

Evil to her very core, Dark Angel delights in destruction and takes pleasure in pain. Though she could have cared less for Hitler's warmongering, the wandering spirit eagerly accepted the Fuhrer's command to kill the Justice Society! Using Paula Von Gunther's magic wand to augment her own powers, Dark Angel trapped the JSA in an enchanted cage.

BLAST HER! SHE HAS MAGICKED HERSELF AWAY!

DARK POWERS

Dark Angel can change her size, teleport, wreak havoc on an individual's appointed place in the timestream, and force weak-willed people, like Hitler's Nazi commandos, to do her evil bidding!

NOW YOU SEE HER...

Green Lantern and Hawkman switched costumes to confuse Dark Angel and destroyed the magic wand imprisoning the Thunderbolt. He in turn freed the JSA. The Nazis were routed... but Dark Angel disappeared into thin air!

93

TORTURER SUPREME
Wonder Woman first encountered Darkseid when the tyrant of Apokolips seized Olympus to usurp the Greek Gods. With Superman's help, Diana thwarted Darkseid, but not before he destroyed the Olympians' hallowed home. Later, Darkseid captured Wonder Woman and directed his master inquisitor Desaad to torture her until she revealed the location of New Olympus.

DARKSEID

IN A TIME long before the Olympians, there existed a race of Old Gods who destroyed themselves in a cataclysmic conflict known as Ragnarok. From that destruction came two worlds, bright and beautiful New Genesis and its dark and bleak twin Apokolips. The dread lord Darkseid soon claimed Apokolips as his own and thereafter waged war on the New Gods of New Genesis in his quest to rule the cosmos. To achieve his dreams of omnipotence, Darkseid has always kept an eye on Earth, suspecting that the powers wielded by its gods and heroes might one day offer him the key to universal dominion.

REAL NAME Darkseid
OCCUPATION Despot
BASE Apokolips
HEIGHT 7 ft 6 in
WEIGHT 515 lb
EYES Red HAIR None
FIRST APPEARANCE
SUPERMAN'S PAL JIMMY OLSEN
#105 (December 1970)

PREMONITION OF DISASTER
Along with Gateway City detective Mike Schorr, Diana escaped Desaad's clutches. She learned from the New God Metron that Darkseid had planned to keep her subdued on Apokolips while he unleashed his shock troops on Themyscira. Diana was allowed a glimpse into Themyscira's grim future!

PARADISE IN RUINS

Traveling via a Boom Tube—the New Gods' teleportation stargate—Diana and Mike Schorr left Apokolips and emerged to find Themyscira battered and burning. They had walked into another trap: Darkseid's Parademons, born and bred for war, swarmed over Wonder Woman while Darkseid watched. Diana single-handedly routed the Apokoliptian army and ceased fighting only when Darkseid grabbed Mike and threatened to crush the detective's skull in his gargantuan grip!

APOKOLIPS NOW!
To spare Mike's life, Darkseid demanded that Diana reveal the location of New Olympus. But to do so would surely spell slavery or death for the gods Diana revered. Darkseid appeared to have the upper hand, until the Amazons, given new hope by Diana's return, launched a counterattack against Darkseid's forces. Darkseid responded by declaring total war on Themyscira and calling down the massive firepower of his Apokoliptian gunships.

DARKSEID'S DEPARTURE
In the end, the lord of Apokolips declared himself suitably impressed by the Amazons' will to fight on in the face of overwhelming odds. Darkseid and his Parademon troops returned to Apokolips through a colossal Boom Tube, leaving more than 1,200 Amazon warriors lying dead.

Unable to stop Darkseid and reeling from the deaths of so many of her Amazon sisters, Diana broke down in the arms of Mike Schorr, who did his best to comfort her.

OUR WORLDS AT WAR
Wonder Woman and Darkseid became uneasy allies during the Imperiex War. Darkseid brought his Apokolips across space to join its energies with Earth and Warworld—then occupied by Superman's android arch-foe Brainiac—to battle the forces of Imperiex. When Brainiac betrayed the alliance and Apokolips's war machinery was destroyed, Diana saw that even mighty Darkseid could be humbled. But with the fate of the universe at stake, Diana convinced the dark god that together they might yet defeat Brainiac and end the war!

ENERGY TRANSFER
Infused by Wonder Woman's spiritual energy, Darkseid created a "transdimensional conduit" by melding his mind with the Atlantean hero Tempest's magical powers. The allies then sent Brainiac back to the dawn of creation to be "dispersed" by the Big Bang.

DIANA'S PARTING GIFT
After the universe was saved, Darkseid was shocked to learn that Diana had infused him with a portion of her peace-loving soul!

ANGLE MAN

...ALWAYS LOOKING FOR THE ANGLE!

ANGELO BEND is a gentleman thief with a unique perspective on crime. Preferring sharp Armani suits and high fashion to tacky, form-fitting spandex costumes, the Angle Man steals what he pleases... but always in *style*. Bend was hired by Barbara Minerva, (formerly the demonic criminal the Cheetah), to heist a priceless and powerful artifact, and he thought he had figured out all the angles to make a clean getaway. However, Donna Troy had a very different viewpoint to the villain's pilfering plans! And Bend could never resist a fetching opponent!

PRECIOUS TREASURE
The Angle Man's prize was the Avatar of Tisiphone, a shard from an ancient vessel created to worship the Furies or "Kindly Ones," a trio of Greek goddesses dedicated to retribution. This fragment was decorated with an image of Tisiphone, the Kindly One who made Helena Kosmatos the host of her power as the World War II heroine known as Fury.

REAL NAME Angelo Bend
OCCUPATION Thief
BASE Mobile
HEIGHT 5 ft 11 in
WEIGHT 175 lb
EYES Brown HAIR Brown
FIRST APPEARANCE
WONDER WOMAN vol. 2 #179
(May 2002)

TROIA'S TRIANGLE TERRORS!

Angelo Bend possesses a triangular apparatus capable of warping space and distorting spatial relationships! It is unclear, however, whether or not the Angle Man's signature weapon is a product of sophisticated science or is some form of mystical talisman. How Bend acquired the triangle is another mystery—he probably stole it. Ever since, he has used it to further his criminal career.

SMOOTH OPERATOR
When the avatar of Tisiphone was forcibly wrenched from Fury's control, Donna Troy set out to help her ailing Amazon sister. After learning of the ancient shard devoted to the Kindly Ones, Donna traveled to Venice, Italy. There, Italian rogue Angelo Bend flirted with her while he sought to make off with the priceless antiquity!

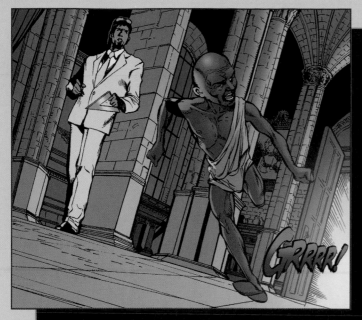

UNMERCIFUL MINERVA

Bending space with his triangle, Angle Man eluded Troia. Ignoring the warnings of the priest Chuma, he travelled to Barbara Minerva's ancestral home in Nottingham, England, expecting to be paid handsomely for obtaining the shard. His payment was much less than he had bargained for, but a big *cut* nonetheless. For Minerva had a special use for the shard—she needed it to get revenge on the rogue who had stolen her Cheetah powers, business mogul Sebastián Ballesteros.

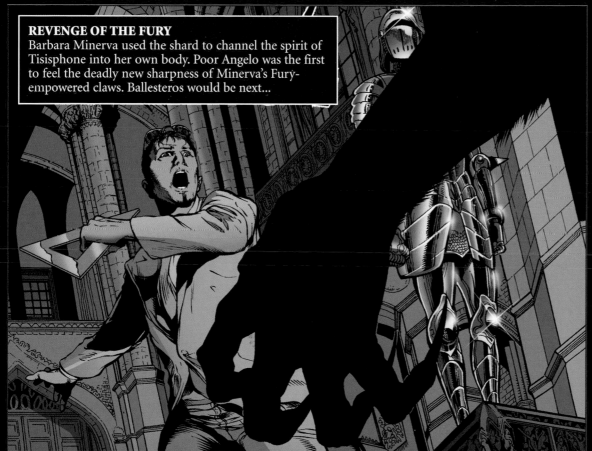

REVENGE OF THE FURY
Barbara Minerva used the shard to channel the spirit of Tisisphone into her own body. Poor Angelo was the first to feel the deadly new sharpness of Minerva's Fury-empowered claws. Ballesteros would be next...

ANGLE MANGLED
Thanks to his space-warping triangle, Angelo escaped Minerva's Nottingham castle. He emerged broken and bleeding on Themyscira —and begging for help.

A DIFFERENT ANGLE
Angle Man's wounds were treated with Amazon medicine on the Isle of Healing. But instead of convalescing, Bend joined Wonder Woman's battle with the Cheetah and his allies in Argentina. While Diana engaged both the new Cheetah and also the vengeful Barbara Minerva, Troia took on the plant-god Urzkartaga, from whom the Cheetah derived his power!

UNLUCKY IN LOVE
Angle Man used his triangle to reveal that the mindbending Dr. Psycho was behind this manifestation of Urzkartaga, and Troia defeated the demented doc. Ailing Angelo still tried to woo her, despite his painful injuries.

DOCTOR PSYCHO

DESPITE HIS DIMINUTIVE SIZE, Doctor Psycho is one of the most powerful foes Wonder Woman has ever faced. The mysterious Doctor murdered and took on the identity of therapist Dr. Charles Stanton, who had been helping Diana's teenage friend Vanessa Kapatelis cope with her best friend's suicide. Disguised as Stanton, Psycho used Vanessa's subconscious as a conduit to attack Wonder Woman and her closest friends on the psychic plane! Although Diana escaped his manipulations, this tiny terror remains a threat to her and to all she holds dear.

THE POWER OF DREAMS
Dr. Psycho's psychic powers enable him to alter and control the perceptions of his victims. Often, he attacks through dreams to create horrific visions of fear and despair. Psycho loves to taunt his victims by entering their hallucinations and assuming any perverted form he wishes!

PSYCHO-DRAMA
Vanessa Kapatelis's fragile mental state made her an ideal pawn. Doctor Psycho continued to mine Vanessa's repressed anger and hurt to have his revenge on Wonder Woman. Then villainous Sébastian Ballesteros hired him to exploit Vanessa's turmoil further, turning her into the Silver Swan, a harpy with a shattering cry!

UNF!

DOCTOR PSYCHO?!

THE DOCTOR IS IN!
Dr. Psycho's most recent encounter with Wonder Woman and her allies occurred in Buenos Aires, Argentina, where the Ballesteros Corporation was headquartered. Dr. Psycho used his abilities to turn Vanessa into The Silver Swan, a bird of prey with a special hatred for Diana. Troia knocked Dr. Psycho unconscious, releasing Vanessa from his thrall. However, Diana learned that Dr. Psycho's damage to Vanessa's mind might have been irreparable.

REAL NAME Unknown
OCCUPATION Psychotherapist
BASE Boston
HEIGHT 3 ft 9 in
WEIGHT 85 lb
EYES Blue HAIR Black
FIRST APPEARANCE
WONDER WOMAN vol. 2 #54
(May 1991)

WHITE MAGICIAN

MONSTER MAKER
Only Randolph himself knew when the spark of goodness inside him was finally extinguished. After the death of Ares Buchanan, the White Magician remained a fixture in the Boston underworld with his own mysterious and sinister agenda.

THOMAS ASQUITH RANDOLPH was once Boston's greatest champion, with a costumed crime-fighting career spanning many decades. In the 1940s, Randolph was the "Mystery Man" known as Mister Magic. Later, he was the White Sorcerer and a member of The Echoes of Justice, a forgotten superhero team. When Wonder Woman came to town, Randolph had settled on "The White Magician" as his arcane alter ego. At first, Diana thought Randolph was an ally helping to defend her adopted city. However, the White Magician was really a pawn of crime lord Ares Buchanan and was about to turn all of his awesome mystical might against her!

> AND I ALWAYS KEEP MY WORD... IT MAKES ME SUCH AN INTERESTING VILLAIN.

REAL NAME
Thomas Asquith Randolph
OCCUPATION Warlock
BASE Boston
HEIGHT 5 ft 11 in
WEIGHT 176 lb
EYES Blue **HAIR** Red
FIRST APPEARANCE
WONDER WOMAN vol. 2 #66
(September 1992)

HIGH LORD DAEMON
Humiliated by Wonder Woman and the Cheetah, Randolph transformed himself into a horned high lord daemon. To attain this level of demonhood, Randolph offered up the Cheetah and his own lover, television news reporter Cassie Arnold, as blood sacrifices to his unholy brethren!

CLAYFACE

BASIL KARLO BELONGS to a select few felons who have dubbed themselves "Clayface." To his credit, the former thespian was the first, an actor-turned-assailant who commemorated his greatest role by making his part as a movie monster a reality. Subsequent Clayfaces, including Matt Hagen, Preston Payne, and the malleable maiden known as Lady Clay, had metahuman morphing abilities and upstaged Karlo's criminal career. Until Karlo stole their combined powers to become—in his own estimation—the "Ultimate Clayface."

RRAAARHH!

FEAT OF CLAY
Basil Karlo usually confined his crimes to Gotham City, home of his foe Batman! But when Karlo learned that Wonder Woman was also molded from enchanted clay, the Ultimate Clayface picked a fight with the Amazing Amazon in New York City, hoping to trap her in his earthen body.

THE NAME IS BASH, BUT PEOPLE CALL ME...
CLAYFACE!

MUD WRESTLING
Karlo succeeded only in absorbing a portion of Diana's substance, but enough to gain godlike power! Clayface regressed Diana in age and stature so that she resembled her younger "spiritual twin" Donna Troy! However, Wonder Woman and Troia masqueraded as one another to fool Clayface and regain Diana's clay. Eventually the sinister shape-shifter was frozen solid for transport back to Gotham's top-security jail Arkham Asylum!

REAL NAME Basil Karlo
OCCUPATION Criminal
BASE Gotham City
HEIGHT 8 ft 7 in
WEIGHT 758 lb
EYES Brown HAIR None
FIRST APPEARANCE
DETECTIVE COMICS #40
(June 1940)

DECAY

LIKE DIANA HERSELF, the demon Decay was brought back to life. To win his father Ares's favor, Phobos, god of fear, journeyed to the Cavern of the Gorgon where he molded a statuette from malevolent matter scoured from Medusa's heart. The statuette came to life and threatened Diana's friend Julia Kapatelis and the city of Boston with death and destruction. Wonder Woman reduced Decay to dust with her golden lasso, but Decay returned to life to inflict rotting ruin upon the world once more!

THE BREATH OF DEATH
Decay's breath seemed to contain the distillation of death itself. Like a cloud of poison gas, this evil exhalation meant certain doom to anything it fell upon. Decay's helpless victims were rapidly reduced into swiftly scattering piles of dust!

Death Touch
Decay's touch also spelled death to all those she grasped. She was invulnerable to all weapons, but she could not resist the life-renewing energy of Wonder Woman's Golden Lasso, which caused her body to explode!

REAL NAME None
OCCUPATION Demon
BASE Cavern of the Gorgons
HEIGHT 6 ft 2 in
WEIGHT 195 lb
EYES Red   HAIR Violet
FIRST APPEARANCE
WONDER WOMAN vol. 2 #3
(April 1987)

IMITATION OF LIFE

Decay was resurrected by Dr. Julian Lazarus's Virtual Reanimator, which brought the demon of destruction back to life with its experimental proto-matrix material. While Decay's body was merely an artificial effigy, the demon's spirit dwelt within! But before Decay could secure the power source needed to maintain her imitation of life, Diana shattered the virtual clone into a million pieces!

ROGUES GALLERY

WONDER WOMAN'S numerous nemeses come from every corner of existence. Ares Buchanan is a god in the guise of man. Lobo is the self-proclaimed "baddest bastich in the known universe!" Mayfly lived life on the razor's edge of evil knowing her time was short. Deathstroke the Terminator vacillated between friend and foe depending on the price. Morgain Le Fay wanted Diana for the very thing she couldn't have. Sinestro was just a puppet on a string, while Egg Fu was truly startling!

ARES BUCHANAN

The War God's enmity for Wonder Woman knows no bounds. Ares once took over the body of Ari Buchanan and raised him up from petty criminal to Boston crimelord. "Ares" Buchanan sired a child with Circe (disguised as assistant D. A. Donna Milton), and brought chaos to Boston's underworld. Ares destroyed his human host in a vain attempt to kill Diana.

LOBO

The so-called "Last Czarnian" annihilated his entire species. His name means "one who devours your entrails and thoroughly enjoys it." This super-strong and self-regenerating intergalactic bounty hunter once enjoyed visiting Earth to brawl with the planet's heroes and heroines. Diana first encountered this alien epitome of random violence during the War of the Gods sparked by Circe.

MAYFLY

Contracted by Ares Buchanan, high-speed hitwoman Mayfly very nearly succeeded in assassinating both Diana and her ally the Flash. Mayfly, who was addicted to the drug Velocity-9 and suffered from a rare form of hemophilia, ended her brief life in prison following her capture by the Amazing Amazon and the Scarlet Speedster.

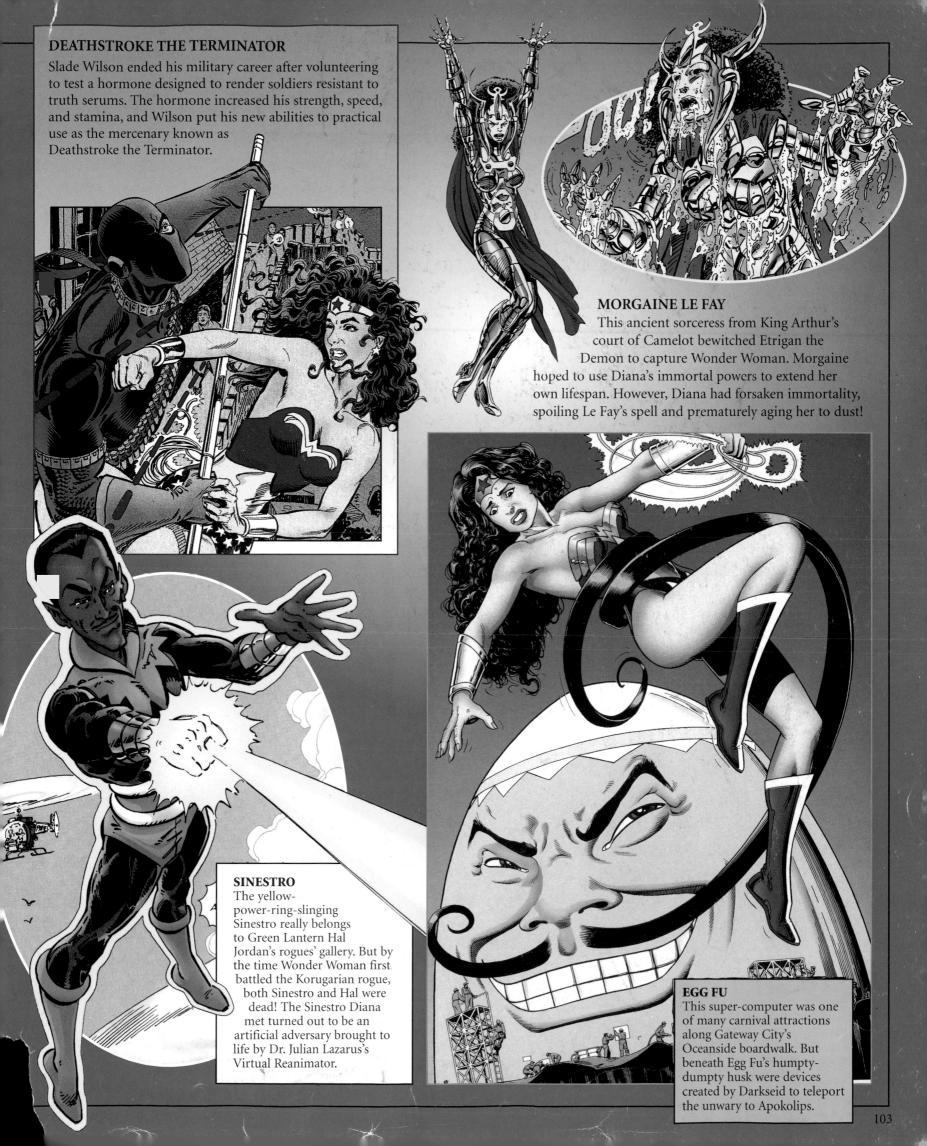

DEATHSTROKE THE TERMINATOR

Slade Wilson ended his military career after volunteering to test a hormone designed to render soldiers resistant to truth serums. The hormone increased his strength, speed, and stamina, and Wilson put his new abilities to practical use as the mercenary known as Deathstroke the Terminator.

MORGAINE LE FAY

This ancient sorceress from King Arthur's court of Camelot bewitched Etrigan the Demon to capture Wonder Woman. Morgaine hoped to use Diana's immortal powers to extend her own lifespan. However, Diana had forsaken immortality, spoiling Le Fay's spell and prematurely aging her to dust!

SINESTRO

The yellow-power-ring-slinging Sinestro really belongs to Green Lantern Hal Jordan's rogues' gallery. But by the time Wonder Woman first battled the Korugarian rogue, both Sinestro and Hal were dead! The Sinestro Diana met turned out to be an artificial adversary brought to life by Dr. Julian Lazarus's Virtual Reanimator.

EGG FU

This super-computer was one of many carnival attractions along Gateway City's Oceanside boardwalk. But beneath Egg Fu's humpty-dumpty husk were devices created by Darkseid to teleport the unwary to Apokolips.

MYTHICAL MONSTERS

GREEK MYTHOLOGY is filled with tales of mythical monsters. Some were the savage children of the gods themselves, others were created by the gods to punish mortals who had dared to anger them. There are one-eyed ogres who would never turn a blind eye to a mortal morsel. There are hybrid horrors of man and beast. And there are creatures whose crimes are so terrible that an eternity in Tartarus is not enough to redeem them. Heroes such as Odysseus and Theseus faced such monstrosities to prove their courage. Wonder Woman has done the same in epic encounters that are already the stuff of legend!

THE CYCLOPES
The giant singled-eyed Cyclopes were sons of Cronus cast down by their cruel father into the depths of Tartarus.

MINOTAUR

The Minotaur was a monster with the head of a bull and the body of a man. Although slain by the Greek hero Theseus, the Minotaur somehow lived on beneath Themyscira's Doom's Doorway, where Diana grappled with the bloodthirsty beast.

MEDUSA

Medusa was one of the three Gorgons, once-beautiful sisters whose hair was turned into serpents by a vengeful goddess. Anyone who looked into the Gorgons' eyes was turned to stone. The Greek hero Perseus slew Medusa and cut off her head. However, Diana met a resurrected Medusa during the contest to choose a new Wonder Woman. Shielding her eyes, Diana dragged Medusa off a high cliff.

BUT WE HAVE ONLY A FEW PRACTICE SPEARS AND WOODEN SWORDS! AND WHAT FELL *BEAST* IS THIS?!

THE HARPIES

The Harpies were believed to be vile goddesses of storms and mischief who flew over battlefields and carried off the weak and wounded. Diana and her Amazon sisters were attacked by Harpies after traveling too close to their Aerie in Themyscira's mystical areas. Diana stayed fended off these malformed maidens and freed her friend Mala from the Harpies' cruel clutches!

HARPIES!

SCYLLA

The six-headed Scylla was one of the terrors faced by the sailor Odysseus and his crew. Some believe Scylla was once a beautiful sea nymph transformed by jealous Circe. In modern times, Diana battled the Scylla on Themyscira, where the creature was loosed by a mysterious foe to terrorize the Amazons!

IXION

Thessaly's King Ixion was the first human to murder a kinsman, his own father-in-law Eioneus. But for the greater sin of desiring Hera, wife of Zeus, Ixion was condemned to be chained to a great wheel in Tartarus for all time—until Ares's child Phobos loosed him upon an unsuspecting Earth!

THE CHIMERA

Part lion, part goat, and part dragon, the fire-breathing Chimera was originally slain by the Greek hero Bellerophon riding upon the winged horse Pegasus. In modern times, the evil children of Ares unleashed the Chimera— among other mythological horrors—upon Gotham City. Wonder Woman managed to subdue the creature using her wits and the Golden Lass___ ___ ok several lead-tipped ar___ ___ Amazon Artemis to fina___ ___ he monster.

ROOWWR

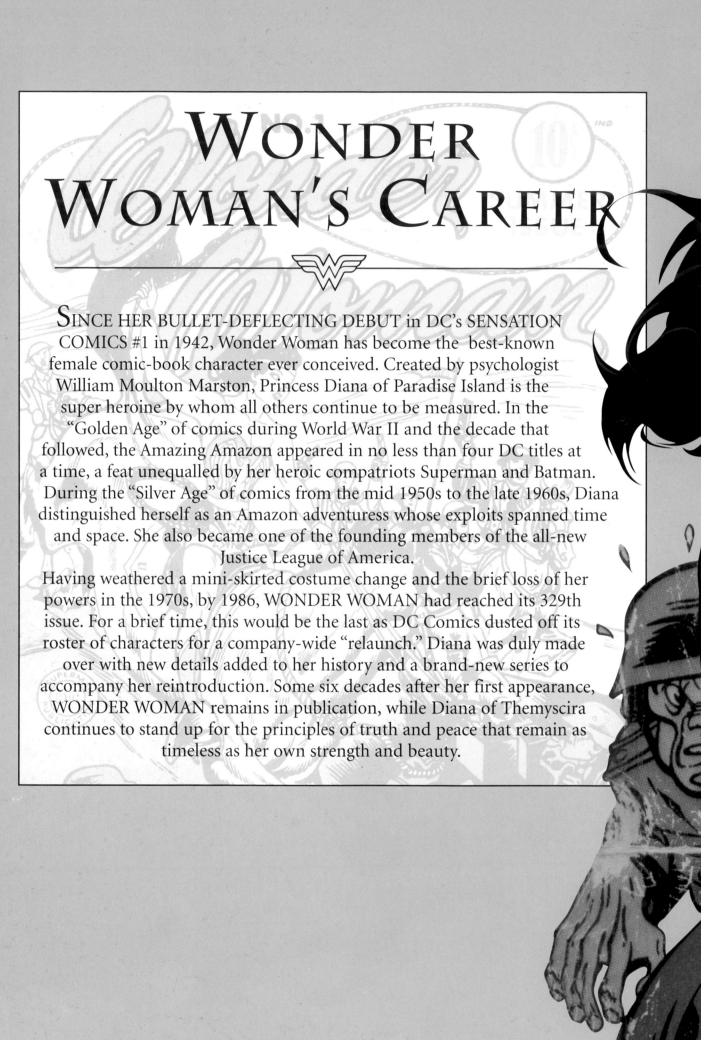

WONDER WOMAN'S CAREER

SINCE HER BULLET-DEFLECTING DEBUT in DC's SENSATION
COMICS #1 in 1942, Wonder Woman has become the best-known
female comic-book character ever conceived. Created by psychologist
William Moulton Marston, Princess Diana of Paradise Island is the
super heroine by whom all others continue to be measured. In the
"Golden Age" of comics during World War II and the decade that
followed, the Amazing Amazon appeared in no less than four DC titles at
a time, a feat unequalled by her heroic compatriots Superman and Batman.
During the "Silver Age" of comics from the mid 1950s to the late 1960s, Diana
distinguished herself as an Amazon adventuress whose exploits spanned time
and space. She also became one of the founding members of the all-new
Justice League of America.
Having weathered a mini-skirted costume change and the brief loss of her
powers in the 1970s, by 1986, WONDER WOMAN had reached its 329th
issue. For a brief time, this would be the last as DC Comics dusted off its
roster of characters for a company-wide "relaunch." Diana was duly made
over with new details added to her history and a brand-new series to
accompany her reintroduction. Some six decades after her first appearance,
WONDER WOMAN remains in publication, while Diana of Themyscira
continues to stand up for the principles of truth and peace that remain as
timeless as her own strength and beauty.

THE GOLDEN AGE

The Amazon Princess as she first appeared. Although she no longer wears long shorts, her costume still looks much as it did more than 60 years ago.

THE GOLDEN AGE of comic books began in the mid-to-late 1930s and extended through the next two decades. During this period many of today's best-known comic-book icons were created. Wonder Woman made her debut in 1941. Though not the first female among the so-called "super heroes" of the era, she is undeniably the most enduring, little changed since her conception. The years that followed saw the introduction of her familiar supporting cast, her recurring Rogues Gallery, and all the details of her abilities and mission.

DIANA PRINCE
The Amazon Princess purchased the identity and credentials of the "real" Diana Prince, a United States Army nurse, and adopted a demure hairstyle and glasses to disguise her appearance.

DIANA'S HAND CLOSES LIKE A STEEL CLAMP ABOUT THE BANDIT'S WRIST---

AMAZON POWERS
Mortal pistol-packing hoodlums were nonplussed by Diana's Herculean strength.

AMAZING AMAZON
The "original" origin of Wonder Woman is only slightly different from her modern one. After U. S. Army pilot Steve Trevor crash-landed on Paradise Island, Aphrodite, Goddess of Love, decreed that the champion of the Amazons should deliver Trevor back to America, the last citadel of democracy, and help fight the forces of hate. Diana, the daughter of Queen Hippolyte, won a contest to choose such an Amazon, and earned the mantle of Wonder W...

WELL, WONDER WOMAN! YOU CAN'T DENY YOUR SERVICES HAVEN'T BEEN RE-QUIRED TO BATTLE CRIME AND INJUSTICE!

THAT'S TRUE, STEVE! AND I'LL BE HAPPY TO KEEP MY PROM-ISE! NOW- WE CAN BE MARRIED!

STEVE TREVOR
If Steve Trevor hadn't crashed on Paradise ... Woman might never have ... ll in love as soon as he set ... es on the Amazon Princess.

HERCULES DEFEATED
Hippolyte's magic girdle made the Amazons unconquerable.

QUEEN HIPPOLYTE

Queen Hippolyte of the Amazons created Diana after learning the art of sculpting a human form from Athena, Goddess of Wisdom. In ancient times, Hippolyte led the Amazons against the armies of Hercules. He seduced her and stole from her Aphrodite's magic girdle. Delivered from slavery by Aphrodite, Hippolyte and her Amazon sisters were forced to abandon man's world to live in peace.

PARADISE ISLAND
By Aphrodite's command, the Amazons left their ancestral Amazonia and journeyed to Paradise Island. Aphrodite also decreed that if any man should set foot on Paradise Island, the Amazons would lose their birthright of eternal life and happiness.

ROBOT PLANE
Wonder Woman left Paradise Island aboard a mentally controlled, indestructible and invisible plane made of "Amazsilikon."

MENTAL RADIO
Wonder Woman may have invented the Mental Radio, which converted brain waves into audio-visual signals. Diana used it to stay in touch with home, as well as her mortal allies,

A KANGA CALLED JUMPA

On Paradise Island, there were no horses to ride. Instead, wild giant kangaroos, or "kangas," roamed free. The Amazons tamed these wonderful animals and rode them in their arena games. In free-for-all rodeo contests, Amazons attempted to lasso each other while mounted on kangas that could leap 50 feet into the air! Diana's favorite kanga was named Jumpa.

Diana displays her prowess at the Amazon sport of "Girl-roping."

HAVE TO EAT IT, ANYWAY—IT'S ALL I HAVE ABOARD

OH-H- IT TASTES LIKE SALTWATER TAFFY.

ETTA CANDY
Woo woo! After Steve Trevor, Wonder Woman's most loyal friend and ally was sweet-toothed Etta Candy. Wonder Woman recruited Etta to round up a hundred pretty girls brave enough to capture dangerous men, thus forming the Holliday Girls of the Holliday College for Women!

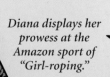

GOLDEN AGE ADVENTURES

THROUGHOUT WORLD WAR II, the Amazon Princess was busy busting spy rings or fighting on the front line against Axis armies. Princess Maru and Baroness Paula Von Gunther were frequent foes. Iron-fisted Mars did whatever he could to fan the flames of war with the help of his evil generals, which included the Duke of Deception, Lord Conquest, and the Earl of Greed. Diana was also menaced by profit-minded mad scientists like Dr. Dirke, who tried to use the wonders of science to do away with her. And if fighting to bring peace to mankind wasn't difficult enough, Wonder Woman often had to fend off otherworldly opponents invading Earth from outer space!

THAT SHRINKING FEELING

The discovery of "Reduso Liquid" promised to make germs so tiny that they could no longer harm humans. Unfortunately, evil Dr. Dirke saw Reduso as a way to miniaturize any nation's army and render it powerless, making the concoction worth millions to countries vying for supremacy. An antidote had to be found!

BATTLE OF THE SEXES

Mars tried time and again to capture Wonder Woman, ordering his generals to do everything in their power. Lord Conquest entered the body of Mammotha, an 8-foot giant loyal to Italian dictator Benito Mussolini. Mammotha offered $5,000 to anyone who could stay in a boxing ring with him for one round.

HERE COME THE TIGEAPES!

The Tigeapes were one of the alien threats Wonder Woman faced when a huge fragment of the planet Neptune crashed into the Pacific Ocean in the winter of 1945. Torn from the Milky Way's eighth planet by tremendous gravitational forces, this "Neptunia" was ruled by the tyrant Solo before Wonder Woman unseated him. Neptunia then became an American protectorate and a useful ally. At Diana's urging, Neptunia adopted an all-female government led by its own Presidenta Una.

ETTA, YOU'RE WONDERFUL!

SURE I AM – I OWE ALL MY SUCCESS TO CANDY!

HOME FREE!

The Earl of Greed scored a double play when he encouraged the treasurer of Holliday College to embezzle the school's coffers! To win the $50,000 necessary to keep the school open, Wonder Woman played baseball with World Series champs the Pups. Not even an explosive baseball thrown by the Earl of Greed could stop the Amazon Princess!

YE—AY—AY! WONDER WOMAN! SHE SHOWED 'EM! HOME RUN! THE PUPS ARE WORLD CHAMPIONS!

DIANA'S GUARDIAN ANGEL

Invited to star in "America's Guardian Angel," a film honoring her spy-catching exploits, Wonder Woman headed for Hollywood. She soon discovered that the motion picture was a scheme by Nazi Baroness Paula Von Gunther to kidnap her. Wonder Woman foiled the plan by mailing her magic lasso to Etta Candy, who hurried to free Diana with the Holliday Girls in tow.

I BROUGHT THE NEW GIRLS, YOUR MAJESTY, AS YOU COMMANDED.

LEAVE THEM—I'LL EXAMINE THEM LATER!

THE MOLE MEN

When Baroness Paula renounced evil, Queen Hippolyte subjected her to several tests, including capturing the Mole Men. This race of underground dwellers painted their female slaves luminous green so that they glowed in the dark!

DOWN MEXICO WAY

Diana Prince and Etta Candy headed south to rescue Etta's brother Mint Candy, from Japanese spies! Wonder Woman saved the famous bullfighter Senorita Pepita— a spy herself— from being trampled by a bull named El Terrifico! The grateful Pepita helped Etta reunite with brother Mint!

INVASION OF THE SUN WARRIORS

On a mission to repair holes in the cosmic dust curtain protecting Earth from the scorching rays of the sun, Wonder Woman discovered that a race of female sun warriors, ruled over by the dazzling Queen Flamina, was streaking towards Earth to conquer mankind!

WARTIME WONDER

Blitzkriegers beware! Although Wonder Woman more often operated in secret, she occasionally used her amazing strength to help out the Allies in battle.

GOLDEN AGE VILLAINS

SHOOT FIRST...
Baroness Paula Von Gunther gets up to her usual tricks.

Dᴜʀɪɴɢ ᴡᴏʀʟᴅ ᴡᴀʀ II and the years that followed, the Amazing Amazon faced a variety of vengeful villains. Woman-hating demigod Hercules resorted to deceit to enslave the Amazon tribe. The Injustice Society connived to carve up the world. Villainy Inc. wanted the same, as long as it meant destroying Wonder Woman, their mutual foe. Nazi agents, such as ruthless Paula Von Gunther, spied for the Third Reich. And while Diana aided the Allies against fascist aggression, invaders from Mars plotted to pick the planet clean.

HERCULES—FROM HERO TO ZERO
Hercules may have been a hero of Greek myth, but to the Amazons, he was the worst of villains. After tricking Hippolyte into removing her golden girdle—a gift from Aphrodite that made the Amazons unconquerable—Hercules and his army enslaved the women warriors. Fortunately, Aphrodite came to their aid and led them to Paradise Island, a place where man was forbidden.

THE INJUSTICE SOCIETY OF THE WORLD

As a member of the Justice Society of America, Wonder Woman often faced the JSA's criminal counterpart, the Injustice Society of the World. The Gambler was a master of disguise; The Brain Wave had hypnotic mental powers; Vandal Savage was an immortal conqueror; The Wizard was a magical menace; Degaton was a time-traveling tyrant; and The Thinker dreamed up schemes using his "thinking cap."

THE BRAIN WAVE

DEGATON

THE GAMBLER

VANDAL SAVAGE

THE WIZARD

THE THINKER

Villainy Incorporated

Villainy Inc. was formed when the Saturnian slave driver Eviless led the escape of her fellow prisoners Giganta, Queen Clea, Byrna Brilyant, Dr. Poison, Hypnota, Zara, and the Cheetah from Transformation Island, the Amazons' confinement area dedicated to criminal rehabilitation. These femme fatales then set their sights on overrunning Paradise Island.

BARONESS PAULA
The Gestapo's chief agent in America, Baroness Paula Von Gunther was a spy and saboteur who would stop at nothing to serve the schemes of Nazi Germany!

AXIS SPIES
In addition to Paula Von Gunther, Wonder Woman battled a number of Axis agents determined to disrupt the Allied War effort, such as Eve Brown and Herr Gross.

Mars, God of War

Warmongering ruler of the red planet, Mars was determined to dominate Earth also. As World War II raged, Mars dispatched his "slave collectors" to collect the souls of fallen soldiers to become servants on his world. Mars's accomplices were the Duke of Deception, Lord Conquest, the Earl of Greed, and General Destruction, his *aide-de-camp*.

THE MASKED MAIDEN
Forced to live in poverty while her rich husband Brutus spent lavishly on hunting trips, Nina Close became the Mask and swore revenge. She bound Brutus, Etta Candy, and the Holliday Girls in acid-filled masks! She then demanded a million dollars in ransom to remove them.

SILVER AGE ADVENTURES

THE SILVER AGE of DC Comics began in 1956 with a general resurgence in the popularity of super heroes. Many comic-book stars of the past were dusted off and reinvented. Wonder Woman received a new artistic direction, while her supporting cast grew to include Wonder Tot and Wonder Girl to tell tales of the Amazon Princess as a toddler and a teen. A revamped Rogues Gallery featured opponents like the Crimson Centipede and Klamos the Conqueror. On the romantic front, Diana's love for Steve Trevor remained unrequited (he only had eyes for Wonder Woman), but the Amazing Amazon was batting them off like flies!

During the Silver Age of comics, Wonder Woman's alter ego Diana Prince continued to serve U. S. Military Intelligence as Col. Steve Trevor's assistant!

STEVE IN SPACE
Col. Steve Trevor's army duties included piloting spacecraft in search of lost rockets. On one trip, he and Wonder Woman discovered dinosaurs on Saturn's moon, Titan!

CURSE OF THE MUMMY
Wonder Woman had crossed paths with Countess Draska Nishki several times in the past. The flame-haired femme fatale returned in 1966 when she marched into Lt. Diana Prince's office and offered her espionage expertise as a spy-for-hire. Naturally, Diana declined. Nishki then tried to sabotage a movie production of *Cleopatra*, starring Diana as the doomed Egyptian queen and Steve Trevor as her beloved, Marc Antony!

BEAUTY AND THE BEAST
In one of many romantic tales, Diana grew tired of the constant marriage proposals of Steve Trevor, Mer-Man, and Bird-Man. Strangely, she agreed to marry "Mr. Monster," a prince from a floating island in the sky.

BOMB DISPOSAL
During the Cold War, Wonder Woman was always on hand to prevent atomic armageddon.

WONDER TOT
Diana's adventures as a toddler were chronicled in a series of Wonder Tot tales. In one of them, she freed "Mr. Genie."

MER-MAN
Half-man, half-fish, Manno was a member of the peace-loving mer-people who lived beneath the waters surrounding Paradise Island. As a teen Mer-Boy, this amorous amphibian often vied for Diana's affections with Bird-Boy. As an adult, Mer-Man occasionally challenged Steve Trevor to prove who was more worthy of Wonder Woman's love.

LOOKING FOR LOVE
Klamos was determined to find the mightiest mate in the universe, so he kidnapped formidable females from across the galaxy, and forced them to fight for the honor! Strangely, Klamos was really a robot!

THE CRIMSON CENTIPEDE
"Make love, not war!" may have been the rallying cry of peace protestors during the turbulent 1960s, but Wonder Woman frequently found herself harassed and harangued by the war god Mars. The Crimson Centipede was specially created by Mars to destroy Diana and spread crime and chaos! With 16 pairs of arms and legs, this creepy-crawly foe packed a passel of punches! Diana squashed this booted bug, and he never returned.

SILVER AGE VILLAINS

WEIRD AND WILD WERE the villains of Wonder Woman's Rogues Gallery during comics' "Silver Age." World-conquering wretches like the Communist Egg Fu now lined up to destroy democracy. Returning rogue the Cheetah reminded Wonder Woman that evil endured in a new decade. As the U. S. and other nations sought to harness the power of the atom, radioactive hysteria fueled fearsome nuclear nemeses like Multiple Man. And as the space race began, Wonder Woman met strange, extra-terrestrial enemies such as amorous alien apes and the Glop, lovesick for the Amazing Amazon. Mysterious monsters such as Boiling Man and the Phantom Sea Beast proved that the Earth's oceans contained a bounty of undiscovered beasts to bedevil Diana!

EGG FU, YUCK!
An egg-shaped creature that threatened to fry the free world with a doomsday rocket, Egg Fu the First was created by the Communist Chinese.

THE CHEETAH
The Cheetah changed her spots for just one adventure, raiding a zoo for a priceless animal to sell to the highest bidder.

BE-BOP-A-LU-GLOP!
The Glop came to Earth in a spaceship camouflaged as a comet. Able to take on the characteristics of anything it digested, the Glop menaced Wonder Girl and young Steve Trevor, gobbling up rockets and bombs. But when the Glop ate a hundred rock'n'roll records, it developed a teenage crush on Wonder Girl!

MULTIPLE MAN

This indestructible nuclear nuisance could transform himself into countless forms. Multiple Man menaced Wonder Woman on many occasions, each time with different superpowers. One bizarre adventure saw Wonder Tot, Wonder Girl, Wonder Woman, and Queen Hippolyte all battling Multiple Man's latest incarnation, a Human Iceberg who threatened to chill the Amazons of Paradise Island into frozen statues!

WONDER WOMAN! -- STOP! -- WE'RE DOOMED! -- SAVE YOURSELF!

GORILLA MY DREAMS!
Animal attraction was certainly at work when Wonder Woman faced a band of space-simians who came to Earth in search of brides. These galactic gorillas transformed the Amazon Princess into an Amazon Primate!

BOILING MAN

Diana met this volcanic villain only once, during Paradise Island's "Name Day." When Boiling Man threatened this annual event, Diana entombed the hot-headed hooligan in an iceberg and tossed him into outer space!

THE PHANTOM SEA BEAST

In another tale featuring the entire Wonder Family at the same time, Wonder Tot, Wonder Girl, Wonder Woman, and Queen Hippolyte were menaced by the Phantom Sea Beast which mysteriously disappeared after encountering each of them. What the Wonder Family didn't realize was that their actions were preventing cruel scientists from transporting this prehistoric monster thousands of years into the future for display in a zoo.

THE MODERN AGE

Forget The Old… the NEW Wonder Woman is here! Thus declared the cover of WONDER WOMAN #178 in 1968 as Diana closed the radical 1960s with her own sweeping changes. As Diana traveled the globe in search of adventure, she did so without Wonder Woman's powers and star-spangled costume, or Steve Trevor, who died tragically. Nevertheless, Diana's devotion to peace was unwavering. The following decade found Diana regaining her abilities and uniform… and even Steve Trevor! As she approached the late 1980s, Wonder Woman proved to everyone that the years 1972 to 1986 had been good to her.

For a time, Diana operated under the tutelage of martial arts master I-Ching, without a costume or superpowers.

WOMEN'S LIBERATION

In one adventure, Wonder Woman learned that Earth's women's liberation movement had inspired a similar movement on the planet Xro. When human feminists began vanishing into thin air, Diana and her JLA teammate Elongated Man discovered a plot by Machsm, High Consul of Xro, to keep the women of his world enslaved.

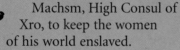

DOCTOR CYBER
Beautiful Dr. Cyber was horribly disfigured when one of her own operatives accidentally threw a brazier of hot coals in her face. She blamed Diana and vowed vengeance!

CATWOMAN'S CLAWS
From Batman's Rogues Gallery, Catwoman joined the ranks of Wonder Woman's feline-inspired foes.

MARS ATTACKS!

Mars made a modern-day appearance when the God of War ignited a conflict between the Amazons of Paradise Island and the denizens of undersea Atlantis!

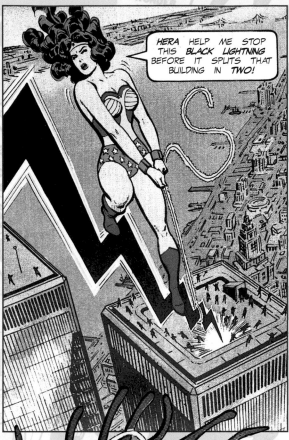

> HERA HELP ME STOP THIS *BLACK LIGHTNING* BEFORE IT SPLITS THAT BUILDING IN *TWO!*

MAXIMUM APPEAL

Beginning in the 1970s, Diana Prince started working at the United Nations. Wonder Woman, meanwhile, tried to ground the black lightning bolts of Maximus, a rich rogue who wanted to kidnap the Amazon Princess, steal her charisma and inject it into himself!

THE GAUCHO

A macho assassin from the South American pampas who rode a flying steed, the Gaucho fought Diana with his electro-lariat and blasting bolas!

THE DUKE OF DECEPTION

Wonder Woman's JLA teammate Green Arrow guest-starred in an adventure, which found the heroes haunted by the hallucinations of Diana's old foe the Duke of Deception! The entire United Nations was in turmoil as the Duke attempted to drive the delegates insane and incite World War III.

RED DRAGON

An explosive encounter with a robot dragon led Wonder Woman and Colonel Steve Trevor to China, where they helped the people thwart a counter-revolutionary called Red Dragon. This warlord intended to overthrow the Chinese government and re-establish the country's bygone feudal system. During one clash, Wonder Woman prevented him from blowing up the Great Wall of China!

IMAGINARY STORIES

WHAT IF THE AMAZON PRINCESS had been raised in 19th-century, Victorian England? How would Wonder Woman battle injustice in a *real* world, where super heroes don't exist? In a cosmic chess game between the gods of Olympus, would order or chaos prevail? The answers can be found in these Imaginary Stories. Whether in "Elseworlds," where the origins of Wonder Woman are recast in surprising ways, or in "Realworld" tales, where fictional super heroes influence all-too-human people, the character of Wonder Woman can bring out the hero in anyone!

AMAZONIA

In this alternate, Victorian reality, women were little more than slaves in a male-dominated society. But the lost race of Amazonia enjoyed peace and prosperity— until Royal Air Marine Steve Trevor washed up on their shores. Trevor feigned friendship while calling down the might of the British Empire. The Amazons were slaughtered, but Trevor spared a single life: Diana, daughter of the Amazons' Queen!

THE WONDER WOMAN

When Diana matured into a beautiful woman, Trevor married her and then forced her to perform in a London stage show as "The Wonder Woman." She used her Amazon abilities to reenact Biblical tales of strong and heroic women.

DESTINY FULFILLED

Diana thwarted an assassination attempt on the American-born King Jack Planters, who had stolen the throne from England's true monarch. Planters was secretly "Jack the Ripper," a bloodthirsty killer who preyed on London's women. Diana ended King Jack's bloody reign and freed women throughout the empire from male oppression.

MATINEE HEROINE

"Realworlds" tales chronicle extraordinary people whose real lives and ambitions intersect with heroes from the DC Universe. Here, up-and-coming actress Brenda Kelly—star of the popular "Wonder Woman" film serials—finds herself embroiled in the Communist witch-hunts of the 1940s.

BUT THE TIME FOR GAMES...

SCREEN KNOCKOUT
Brenda's Wonder Woman is a hit battling the Baroness and other Nazis in movie serials. But reality proves rather more complex!

IS OVER!

CLARK KENT: SUPER-CENTAUR!
Unable to prevent the Ares-controlled Nazis from incinerating Metropolis with a bomb, the Man of Steel is turned into a Super-Centaur cavorting with the Maenads, devotees of Dionysus, God of Wine. Only the love of his childhood sweetheart, Lana Lang, can free Clark from this spell.

LOIS LANE: SUPER HERO!
Empowered by Artemis and other noble gods, reporter Lois Lane is transformed into a Wonder Woman!

WHOM GODS DESTROY

In this tale, a faction of the gods of Olympus decides to take an active part in the affairs of mankind. Led by Ares, these gods meddle with humanity's fate by propping up Nazi Germany, which has *won* World War II and now rivals the United States as a nuclear superpower. Into this highly volatile world comes Superman; however, he is quickly defeated by the allies of Ares. Wonder Woman remains humanity's only hope of avoiding world war and achieving lasting peace.

ROLE REVERSAL
But if Lois Lane is Wonder Woman, where is Diana? Unfortunately, in this "Elseworld" story, the Amazon Princess is a Nazi warrior utterly loyal to Ares and busily stoking the fires of war!

TIMELINE

THE PRINCESS OF PEACE entered Patriarch's World in 1941, and not a moment too soon. With the Allied nations locked in battle with Axis aggressors, Wonder Woman's creation during World War II gave many comic-book readers of all ages and from every walk of life hope that truth and liberty might yet prevail over tyranny. More than six decades later, Diana's mission is as important as ever. With her star-spangled costume, bullet-deflecting bracelets, and magic lasso, the Amazing Amazon continues to illustrate that love and unity are worth fighting for most of all.

1941

Winter: **Wonder Woman**, **Queen Hippolyte**, the **Amazons of Paradise Island**, and **Steve Trevor** are all introduced to comic-book readers in a brief, 8-page tale appearing in DC Comics' ALL-STAR COMICS #8.

1942

January: Wonder Woman makes comic-book history with her full-length, bullet-deflecting debut in DC's SENSATION COMICS #1! In this issue, Wonder Woman purchases the name and credentials of **Diana Prince**, a U. S. Army nurse, thus assuming her longtime secret identity. Diana's Amazon plane is introduced in this issue as a propeller-driven aircraft. In 1956, the plane will become a sleek jet.

February: **Etta Candy** and the **Holliday Girls** sorority of Holliday College are introduced as Wonder Woman encounters her first costumed foe, **Princess Maru**, also known as the diabolical **Dr. Poison**! (SENSATION COMICS #2)

March: Steve Trevor's superior and Diana Prince's boss **Colonel** (later General) **Darnell** is introduced. Darnell harbors a secret affection for Diana. Also this issue, Wonder Woman matches wits with the Nazi spy known as **Herr Gross**! (SENSATION COMICS #3)

April: Ruthless Axis agent **Baroness Paula Von Gunther** debuts. She will become Wonder Woman's most persistent foe during World War II. (SENSATION COMICS #4)

Summer: The Amazing Amazon is awarded her own self-titled comic book series, beginning with a titanic 64-page issue featuring **Hercules** and the **Gods of Olympus**! Also this issue, Diana encounters Japanese spy **San Yan**. (WONDER WOMAN #1)

June: Wonder Woman first wields her magic golden lasso, a gift from Queen Hippolyte, in an issue that introduces the Amazon sport of "girl-roping" while riding giant kangas. (SENSATION COMICS #6)

June–July: Wonder Woman joins the **Justice Society of America** for a wartime adventure. (ALL-STAR COMICS #11)

The Amazons' origins were recounted in the debut issue of WONDER WOMAN. Diana also battled Paula Von Gunther, went to the circus, and roped a raging bull with her lasso!

July: After attempting to monopolize America's milk supply, Paula Von Gunther is executed in the electric chair for her crimes. She is later brought back to life thanks to one of her own diabolical inventions. (SENSATION COMICS #7)

August–September: Diana is asked to become the JSA's official secretary. (ALL-STAR COMICS #12)

Kanga-what? Native to Paradise Island, giant kangas like the one Diana rode in SENSATION COMICS #6 could leap 50 feet into the air and were ridden in the Amazons' gladiatorial games.

On the first comic-book cover to feature Wonder Woman, the Amazing Amazon is shown defending Capitol Hill from the forces of organized crime.

The "Mystery Men" of the Justice Society of America form a "V" for victory against the Axis powers with the team's first female member, Wonder Woman!

September: Wonder Woman adds Axis spy **Agent X** to her Rogues Gallery. Also this issue, Wonder Woman meets the real Diana Prince once again and battles **Dr. Cue**. (SENSATION COMICS #9)

Fall: Wonder Woman battles the **Duke of Deception, Lord Conquest,** and the **Earl of Greed,** commanders of the war god **Mars** (formerly **Ares**). (WONDER WOMAN #2)

October–November: Wonder Woman meets Venusian **Queen Desira** when the JSA are "Shanghaied Into Space!" (ALL-STAR COMICS #13)

Winter: With the release of COMIC CAVALCADE #1, Wonder Woman now appears in four regular comic book publications! In this issue, Diana catches the crook and fifth-columnist known as **Mr. Kipp.**

1943

January: With her traditional costume missing, Diana dons a red-and-green ensemble—complete with black domino mask—in the pages of SENSATION COMICS #13, in which Wonder Woman battles the onerous **Olga**, yet another Nazi spy!

February–March: Wonder Woman rescues Baroness Paula Von Gunther's daughter **Gerta** and other children from a Nazi death camp. Like her mother, Gerta later menaces Diana on several occasions. But in this issue, Paula herself begins her rehabilitation, supervised by the statuesque **Mala** on the Amazons' Reform Island. Paula dedicates her life to Aphrodite and later becomes Wonder Woman's loyal ally. (WONDER WOMAN #3)

March: Nazi collaborator **Simon Slikery** joins Wonder Woman's roster of alliterative adversaries. (SENSATION COMICS #15)

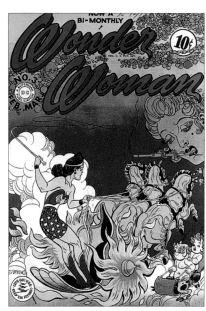

Driving Apollo's sun-chariot, Diana faces her Nazi nemesis Baroness Paula Von Gunther on the cover for WONDER WOMAN #3. Inside the comic book, however, no such scene exists.

Spring: Wonder Woman foils Nazi agent **Fausta Grables**! (COMIC CAVALCADE #2)

April: Oh no! Diana unfortunately breaks Etta Candy's heart when she reveals that Etta's fiancé **Karl Schultz** is a Gestapo agent in cahoots with Japan! (SENSATION COMICS #16)

April–May: Wonder Woman battles both **Blakfu**, the king of the **Mole Men**, and rubber magnate **Ivar Torgson** in the pages of WONDER WOMAN #4!

May: Diana encounters **Princess Yasmini**, a Hindu spy who commits suicide rather than betray her spy ring. (SENSATION COMICS #17)

June: Wonder Woman meets the evil Inca priest known as **Quito**! (SENSATION COMICS #18)

June–July: Diana encounters **Dr. Psycho,** who plots to return American women to "clanking chains and abject captivity." (WONDER WOMAN #5)

Hail to the Chief! Wonder Woman was way ahead of her time when she ran for President of the United States against Steve Trevor in the far-flung future!

July: While captured by the kidnapper **Mavis** (a former slave of Paula Von Gunther), Wonder Woman is robbed of her bracelets and runs amok until Paula ropes Diana with her own magic lasso and her gauntlets are restored in SENSATION COMICS #19. This issue introduces the concept that Amazons are driven mad if their bracelets of submission are removed.

August: Diana thwarts the Nazi spy **Stoffer**! (SENSATION COMICS #20)

September: In his first and last appearance, master criminal **American Adolf** chooses death before dishonor when his plot to conquer the United States is thwarted by Wonder Woman. (SENSATION COMICS #21)

Fall: Schizophrenic socialite **Priscilla Rich** first dons the costume of that "treacherous, relentless huntress," **Cheetah**! (WONDER WOMAN #6)

November: Bully **Mugsy McGrew** discovers that Diana has "a jaw like a battleship," and Diana sends Steve Trevor a "mental radio message." (SENSATION COMICS #23)

Elsewhere, Wonder Woman takes on the femme fatale **Bertha Nagle**! (COMIC CAVALCADE #4)

Winter: Wonder Woman runs for President of the United States against President-elect Steve Trevor and *wins… albeit in 3004!* In this fanciful tale, Diana and Hippolyte peer into the future via the Amazons' magic sphere! (WONDER WOMAN #7)

Also, Diana first meets the evil **Zara**, high priestess of the Cult of the Crimson Flame. (COMIC CAVALCADE #5)

December: Inspired by Aphrodite, Wonder Woman controls her Invisible Plane by "mental radio." (SENSATION COMICS #24)

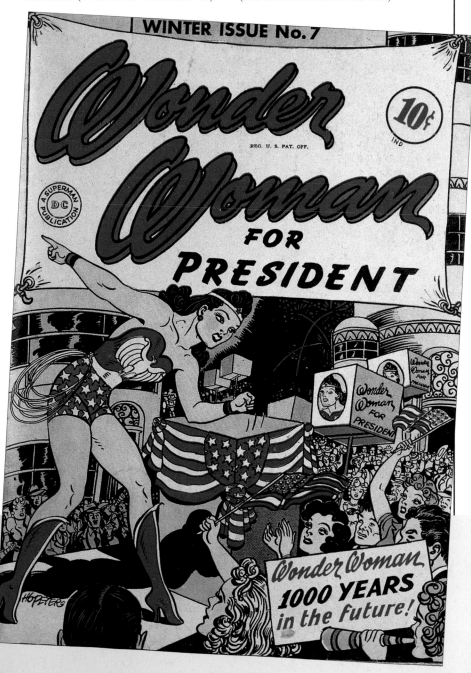

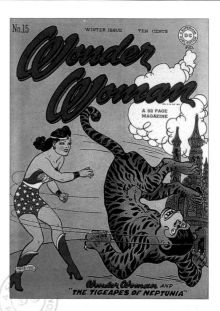

Part-tiger, part-monkey, the fantastical Tigeapes were one of many alien adversaries Diana faced throughout her early comics career.

Diana's magic lasso didn't just make criminals tell the truth. She could use her unbreakable lariat to rope gun-toting gangsters!

1944
February: To prevent a premonition of Diana's murder coming true, Hippolyte masquerades as a domino-masked Wonder Woman, even wrestling with the real Amazing Amazon in a tale of double identity! (SENSATION COMICS #26)

March: Wonder Woman prevents businessman **Ely Close** from stealing a top-secret alternative automobile fuel! (SENSATION COMICS #27)

Spring: Wonder Woman meets the evil **Queen Clea** and the Amazons of sunken Atlantis! (WONDER WOMAN #8)

Elsewhere, Diana's first encounter with **Countess Mazuma** is chronicled in COMIC CAVALCADE #6.

April: Wonder Woman battles civic corruption in the form of **Police Chief Smack** and **Mayor Prude**! (SENSATION COMICS #28)

May: Wonder Woman meets the malicious **Mimi Mendez**! (SENSATION COMICS #29)

June: Wonder Woman finds herself in the mystic grasp of cult leader **Anton Unreal**! (SENSATION COMICS #30)

Summer: Diana first grapples with **Giganta**, a female gorilla scientifically transformed by **Professor Zool**'s electronic evolutionizer into a redheaded rogue! (WONDER WOMAN #9)

Also, Diana fends off the terrible talons of **The Vulture King**! (COMIC CAVALCADE #7)

August: Wonder Woman first encounters **The Crime Chief**! (SENSATION COMICS #32)

Fall: The sadistic Saturnian slave-driver **Eviless** is introduced in WONDER WOMAN #10; however she is not mentioned by name until WONDER WOMAN #28. Also in WONDER WOMAN #10, Diana battles scheming spy **Duke Mephisto Saturno** no less than three times in as many tales!

Elsewhere, Diana catches the criminal known as **Casino** in COMIC CAVALCADE #8!

October: Yet another public official goes bad when Wonder Woman battles the ironically named **Mayor Goode**! (SENSATION COMICS #34)

November: Diana meets the sinister **Sontag Henya** in Atlantis! (SENSATION COMICS #35)

December: Wonder Woman first battles **Bedwin Footh**! (SENSATION COMICS #35)

Winter: Diana meets two new villainesses: **Neptune** in COMIC CAVALCADE #9, and **Hypnota the Great** in WONDER WOMAN #11!

1945
March: **Nero** becomes Wonder Woman's new nemesis. (SENSATION COMICS #39)

Spring: Diana battles **The Great Blue Father**. (COMIC CAVALCADE #10)

April: Wonder Woman finds a deadly new foe in **Countess Draska Nishki**! (SENSATION COMICS #40)

Summer: Diana meets the evil **King Rigor** and his **Seal Men**! (WONDER WOMAN #13)

September: **Amazsilikon** is introduced as the material comprising Diana's Invisible Plane. Also this issue, Diana meets and befriends the eight-foot-tall **Marya** the mountain girl! (SENSATION COMICS #45)

Fall: In COMIC CAVALCADE #12, Wonder Woman first fights **Dalma**, while WONDER WOMAN #14 introduces the Amazing Amazon to **The Gentleman Killer**!

October: **The Lawbreakers' Protective League** proves to be no match for Wonder Woman. (SENSATION COMICS #46)

November: Diana thwarts the murderous intentions of **The Unknown**, the alter ego of **Mr. Pipsqueak**! (SENSATION COMICS #47)

December: Wonder Woman takes on the team of **Topso and Teena**. (SENSATION COMICS #48)

Winter: In separate tales, Wonder Woman battles **Solo** and tangles with the simian-headed and feline-bodied **Tigeapes of Neptune** in WONDER WOMAN #15, later taking on gambler and racketeer **Paltro Debum** in COMIC CAVALCADE #13.

1946
April: Wonder Woman first encounters **Professor Toxino**. (SENSATION COMICS #52)

April–May: Diana triumphs over Holliday College social climber-turned-criminal **Wanta Wynn**. (COMIC CAVALCADE #14)

June: Wonder Woman discovers that **Dr. Fiendo** skipped his Hippocratic oath! (SENSATION COMICS #54)

June–July: Diana meets the unscrupulous **Uriah Skinflint**. (COMIC CAVALCADE #15)

Fall: Buzzing **Bughumans** plague the Amazing Amazon! (SENSATION COMICS #55)

September: Wonder Woman battles the mad, hatchet-wielding **Syonide**. (SENSATION COMICS #57)

September–October: Diana thwarts Supreme Leader **Blitz**! (WONDER WOMAN #19)

October–November: Diana battles Norse god Odin's daughter **Gundra** and the **Valkyries** of Norse myth in COMIC CAVALCADE #17.

November: Wonder Woman first encounters the evil **Blue Snow Man**, who is actually the female **Byrna Brilyant** in disguise! (SENSATION COMICS #59)

November–December: Traveling back through time to ancient Rome, Wonder Woman meets **Julius Caesar**! Also in this issue, Diana clips the wings of **Nifty** and her all-female **Air Pirates**! As well, Holliday College faculty member **Prof. Chemico** is introduced. Chemico's fabrications will become frequent plot devices. (WONDER WOMAN #20)

1947
January–February: Wonder Woman battles **Atomia,** queen of the Atomic Kingdom U-235! (WONDER WOMAN #21)

March: In "The Wail of Doom!" Wonder Woman battles **Professor Vibrate,** a physics teacher at Holliday College who has his own gang of bank robbers! (SENSATION COMICS #63)

March–April: Diana sees green on the planet Venus when she defeats the aptly named **Gell Osey**! (WONDER WOMAN #22)

June–July: It's another oceanic adventure when Diana swims after **Queen Sharkeeta,** a mermaid with the body of a shark! (COMIC CAVALCADE #21)

July–August: Diana encounters raven-haired villainess **Nina Close, The Mask**! Nina is really a mousy blonde. (WONDER WOMAN #24)

November–December: Journeying close to the sun, Wonder Woman and the Holliday Girls meet **Queen Celerita** and the **Speed Maniacs from Mercury**! (WONDER WOMAN #26)

1948
February: Wonder Woman puts international jewel smuggler **Spud Spangle** out of business! (SENSATION COMICS #74)

February–March: Diana meets her match in the superpowered **Badra,** an evil alien thief from the planet Hator. Also in this issue, Reform Island is henceforth referred to as **Transformation Island.** (COMIC CAVALCADE #25)

March–April: In the classic, "**Villainy Incorporated**" tale, Diana combats a confederation that comprises eight of her very worst foes, namely Eviless, Cheetah, Queen Clea, Dr. Poison, Zara, Hypnota, Giganta, and Byrna Brilyant. (WONDER WOMAN #28)

April: Readers meet **Jumpa,** Diana's favorite kanga on Paradise Island! (SENSATION COMICS #76)

May–June: Diana gets a chilly reception when she meets **Prime Minister Blizzard**! (WONDER WOMAN #29)

July–August: Wonder Woman thwarts the jealous **Mona Menise,** who has been endowed with the seductive powers of the Sirens and has set her sights on winning Steve Trevor! (WONDER WOMAN #30)

September: Diana encounters the despicable **Dr. Frenzi**! (SENSATION COMICS #81)

1949
January–February: Wonder Woman thwarts the insidious schemes of **Inventa,** who succeeds in escaping from Transformation Island! (WONDER WOMAN #33)

February: Diana find a new avaricious adversary in **C. O. Lector,** a millionaire who covets Wonder Woman's Amazon bracelets! (SENSATIONS COMICS #86))

July–August: Diana meets **Astra,** youthful queen of the planet Infanta, an ally who will later help Wonder Woman to defeat the Duke of Deception in deep space! (WONDER WOMAN #36)

September–October: Wonder Woman first encounters the enchantress **Circe.** (WONDER WOMAN #37)

November–December: DC's SENSATION COMICS briefly alters its style and substance, adding "**Dr. Pat**" and "**Romance, Inc.**" features to supplement the lighter Wonder Woman lead stories featuring Princess Diana's deft deflecting of Steve Trevor's frequent marriage proposals. (SENSATION COMICS #94)

1950
March–April: Socialite **Tora Rivvers** plots sabotage when denied the lead role in *Hollywood Goes to Paradise Island.* (WONDER WOMAN #40)

March–April: Diana agrees to marry Steve Trevor, but only if he picks Diana Prince over Wonder Woman. Steve chooses Wonder Woman and misses out on marital bliss! (SENSATION COMICS #96)

May–June: Wonder Woman becomes Romance Editor of the *Daily Globe* newspaper. Contemplating Steve Trevor's proposals, Diana consults Aphrodite's Law, which says that she must give up being an Amazon and forfeit her lasso, bracelets, and Invisible Plane if she chooses marriage over battling injustice. (SENSATION COMICS #97)

July–August: Diana prevents interstellar invader **General Vertigo** from conquering Earth. (WONDER WOMAN #42)

November–December: In "Monarch of the Sargasso Sea," Diana meets the maniacal **Master De Stroyer.** (WONDER WOMAN #44)

Elsewhere, in SENSATION COMICS' centennial issue, Wonder Woman thwarts criminals **Igor Gorgo** and **Zita Zanders**!

Diana helped to harness the power of the atom when she battled Queen Atomia. The Queen reformed and resolved to help humanity after Aphrodite welded a magic Venus girdle around her waist! Seriously!

As SENSATION COMICS took a more romantic approach to storytelling, Diana found Steve Trevor proposing matrimony at every turn!

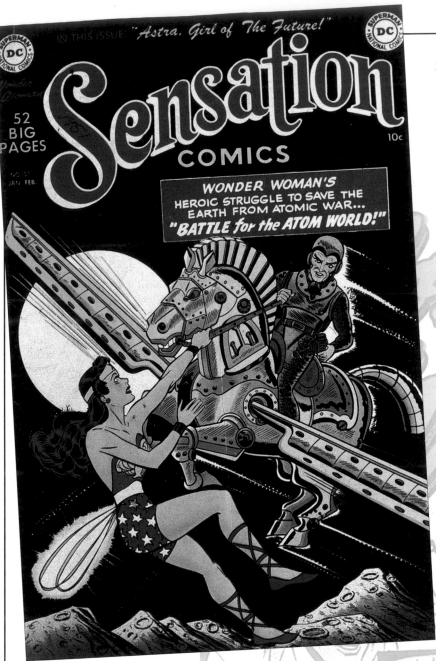

Fact met fiction when Wonder Woman was tested with the lie detector, the other famous invention by her creator, William Moulton Marston.

The diabolical Professor Luxo tried to bring America to its knees by sabotaging atomic energy projects under Steve Trevor's supervision!

1951

January–February: Diana prevents **Professor Luxo** from conquering America with atomic tampering. (SENSATION COMICS #101)

February–March: ALL-STAR COMICS goes on an extended hiatus with its 57th issue, ending its run with Wonder Woman and her fellow JSAers solving "The Mystery of the Vanishing Detectives!" ALL-STAR will return in March 1976 and continue with an all-new JSA lineup sans Wonder Woman until issue #74 in October 1978, when it ceases publication for good.

March–April: After grappling with **The Grenade Gang**, Diana meets two more academic adversaries when she matches wits with **Professor Turgo** and **Professor Jenkel** in separate stories! (WONDER WOMAN #46)

May: In the far-flung future, Wonder Woman encounters the evil **Proto**, a 20th-century, time-travelling scientist who has journeyed to the year 2051 in order to become the dictator of New Metropolo, formerly known as New York City! (SENSATION COMICS #103)

September–October: In the land of Mu, Diana grapples with the evil **Prince Ghu**, and later battles **The Boss**! (WONDER WOMAN #49)

November–December: Wonder Woman makes her final appearance in SENSATION COMICS. (SENSATION COMICS #106)

Elsewhere, Diana once more encounters a sinister spy—this time it's that master of disguise **General Voro**—as WONDER WOMAN reaches its milestone 50th issue!

1952

January–February: Diana grapples with the gang leader known as **Garo**. (WONDER WOMAN #51)

March–April: Amazonium, the "hardest metal known," is first mentioned as the alloy of Wonder Woman's bracelets of submission and, later, also her royal tiara. Also this issue, Diana battles **Prime Minister Zago** and the wizard **Strogo** in separate stories. (WONDER WOMAN #52)

May–June: In a nod to her creator William Moulton Marston, the inventor of the lie detector, Wonder Woman is pictured taking a polygraph test and being interrogated about her secret identity on the cover of WONDER WOMAN #53. Also this issue, Diana takes on **The Crime Master of Time**!

November–December: Organized crime takes a battering when Diana meets and defeats **The Nestor Brothers** and **The Plotter Gang** in separate tales. (WONDER WOMAN #56)

1953

January–February: In 15th century Italy, Diana thwarts diabolical **Duke Perilosa**. Also this issue, Wonder Woman battles the **Mole Men**! (WONDER WOMAN #57)

March–April: The world threatens to crumble apart unless Wonder Woman can defeat the **Termite Queen** and her invading armies of termites! In other tales, the Amazing Amazon thwarts both **Brain** and the sun-stealing **Phaethon**. (WONDER WOMAN #58)

May–June: Diana defeats **Duke Dazam**, ruler of a parallel Earth. (WONDER WOMAN #59)

September–October: In separate stories, Wonder Woman takes on **Troglodytes** and Bourabian baddie **Zoxab**! (WONDER WOMAN #61)

November–December: Diana deposes underworld leader **Angles Andrews**, (who is no relation to her future adversary Angle Man). (WONDER WOMAN #62)

1954

January: The Amazing Amazon encounters **The Human Tank** and later time-travels to 16th-century Sardonia to battle **Prince Rupert**. (WONDER WOMAN #63)

February: Wonder Woman fights a war of wills with **The Thought Master**! (WONDER WOMAN #64)

November: Wonder Woman first encounters smooth-talking professional criminal **Angelo Bend**, a.k.a. **Angle Man**! Also in this issue, Wonder Woman's golden lasso is mistakenly described as being forged from **Amazonium**, and she matches wits with **Professor Uxo** and the **Volcano Prophet** in separate tales. (WONDER WOMAN #70)

1955

February: Wonder Woman meets the bizarre **Mole Goldings**, utterly annihilating the gilded Mole people when they attempt to invade Earth from beneath its crust! (WONDER WOMAN #72)

April: Diana clashes with the **Prairie Pirates**! (WONDER WOMAN #73)

July: Not to be confused with Angle Man, the gangster **Angler** tries to discover Wonder Woman's secret identity. (WONDER WOMAN #75)

August: Wonder Woman traverses time to thwart **Duke Naxok**! (WONDER WOMAN #76)

October: There's no clean getaway for **The Smokescreen Gang** when they meet the Amazing Amazon! (WONDER WOMAN #77)

November: WONDER WOMAN #78 includes the last mention to date of Diana's job as Romance Editor for the *Daily Globe.*

1956
January: Wonder Woman is shrunken to miniscule size and battles killer fleas in her first and only battle with the criminal **Spider!** (WONDER WOMAN #79)

February: "The Origin of the Amazon Plane" reveals the trials of Diana to retrieve and assemble the components of her Invisible Plane. Also this issue, Wonder Woman meets criminal mastermind **Machino**, who locks a bomb-laden mask on her face! (WONDER WOMAN #80)

No rest for the not-at-all wicked! Mad bomber Machino clamped an explosive facemask on Diana while she was taking a nap! Unable to take off the mask, Diana made Machino deactivate the bomb.

May: A time warp permits Diana the first of several meetings with **Robin Hood and his Merry Men!** (WONDER WOMAN #82)

August: Wonder Woman uproots **The Plant People** in "The Tree That Shook the Earth!" (WONDER WOMAN #84)

October: In separate tales within WONDER WOMAN #85, Diana meets and defeats both **Duke Bale** and **Captain Virago!**

November: Diana stops **The Snatcher** from snatching her Invisible Plane! (WONDER WOMAN #86)

1957
July: Wonder Woman wins the Interplanetary Olympics! (WONDER WOMAN #91)

October: Diana thwarts undersea Mermen, no relation to her later teenage crush **Mer-Boy.** (WONDER WOMAN #93)

1958
January: Diana fights the evil extraterrestrial **Phenegs** in a story that suggests that her Amazon tiara was a gift from an alien scientist in return for turning back a Pheneg invasion! (WONDER WOMAN #95)

May: The "modern age" Hippolyte makes her first appearance. (WONDER WOMAN #98)

July: Wonder Woman stops **The Silicons** from shattering Earth with their artificial comets. (WONDER WOMAN #99)

August: WONDER WOMAN #100 marks a major milestone for Princess Diana as her centennial issue is sealed inside a time capsule on Paradise Island for future generations!

October: In "The Fun House of Time!" Diana matches wits with **The Time Master.** (WONDER WOMAN #101)

1959
January: Diana grapples with the genius **Gadget-Maker.** (WONDER WOMAN #103)

April: In "The Secret Origin of Wonder Woman," Diana's origin is revised, revealing that she was instead the daughter of human parents with powers granted by the gods. (WONDER WOMAN #105)

July: Diana's adventures as a teenaged **Wonder Girl** are first chronicled as she meets the lovestruck Mer-Boy—a frequent guest star later—and earns her eagle-emblazoned costume. Wonder Girl receives top-billing on many WONDER WOMAN covers afterward. Also this issue, Wonder Woman duels with space-faring gunslingers **Ronnkn** and **Zgggm!** (WONDER WOMAN #107)

November: The Amazon Princess encounters the robotic **Princess No. 1003**, whose sudden visit to Earth nearly sparks off an interplanetary war! (WONDER WOMAN #110)

1960
January: In his first appearance, the cunning **Professor Menace** creates a Wonder Woman robot to replace the real Amazing Amazon. (WONDER WOMAN #111)

March: Wonder Woman teams with male super heroes Aquaman, The Flash, Green Lantern and the Martian Manhunter to defeat **Starro the Conqueror**, an alien starfish. Together, these five champions form **The Justice League of America!** (THE BRAVE AND THE BOLD #28)

April: Diana prevents the once-mummified 7,000-year-old **Queen Mikra** from conquering the world with her stone sphinxes! (WONDER WOMAN #113)

November: Wonder Woman now fights evil twice monthly as the JLA appears in its own title with JUSTICE LEAGUE OF AMERICA #1. Diana will remain the team's sole female member until **Hawkgirl** (**Shayera Thal**) joins in JUSTICE LEAGUE OF AMERICA #31.

Also this month, **Mer-Man Manno** (former teenage sweetheart Mer-Boy) swims back into Diana's life to rival Steve Trevor for her affections. (WONDER WOMAN #118)

In her milestone 100th issue, Wonder Woman used Professor Alpha's X-Dimension machine to visit a strange other-dimensional realm populated by gargantuan forest giants and her own identical twin!

In addition to perennial paramours Mer-Man and Steve Trevor, the amorphous yet strangely amorous Amoeba-Man added himself to Diana's list of suitors in WONDER WOMAN #125. He turned out to be an evil extraterrestrial invader!

1961

May: Wonder Woman battles yet another Saturnian foe, **The Sinister Seer!** (WONDER WOMAN #122)

July: Diana's exploits as an Amazonian toddler begin with the introduction of **Wonder Tot!** (WONDER WOMAN #122)

August: Paradoxically, Wonder Tot, Wonder Girl, Wonder Woman, and Hippolyte (**Wonder Queen,** naturally) all appear in the same impossible tale which introduces the atomic explosion-spawned **Multiple Man!** (WONDER WOMAN #124)

October: A mystery is resolved! Wonder Woman's Invisible Plane is now described as being fabricated from "elastic Amazonium." (WONDER WOMAN #125)

1962

January: Diana battles Planet K's **Kuu-Kuu** and his alien invasion force. (WONDER WOMAN #127)

February: The secrets of Wonder Woman's fantastic Invisible Jet are explored in "The Origin of the Amazing Robot Plane!" This tale claims that Diana's plane is actually the mythical winged steed **Pegasus,** miraculously transformed into an aircraft. (WONDER WOMAN #128)

Also this month, flashbacks reveal how the JLA came together on its first case, battling an alien menace that transforms people into objects. (JUSTICE LEAGE OF AMERICA #9

November: Diana faces up to the insidious **Image-Maker!** (WONDER WOMAN #134)

1963

February: The mechanical **Machine Men** attempt to transform Diana into a giantess in order to make her an outcast and clear the way for their conquest of Earth! (WONDER WOMAN #136)

September–October: In "The Academy of Arch-Villains," Wonder Woman grapples with Angle Man, and two new foes, **Mouse Man** and **Fireworks Man,** each eager to win the underworld's Golden WW statue for capturing and/or destroying the Amazon Princess! (WONDER WOMAN #141)

1964

January–February: Wonder Girl finds herself caught in an amorous tug-o'-war between Mer-Boy and a new suitor, **Bird-Boy!** (WONDER WOMAN #144)

March–April: In yet another impossible tale, the entire Wonder Family battles **The Phantom Sea-Beast!** (WONDER WOMAN #145)

1965

January: Wonder Girl meets **The Glop,** an alien from outer space who learns English by ingesting 100 rock-and-roll records! Crazy, man! (WONDER WOMAN #151)

June–July: **Donna Troy** is introduced as **Wonder Girl,** adopted sister of Wonder Woman! Wonder Girl joins the **Teen Titans** (Robin, Kid Flash, and Aqualad) this issue. (THE BRAVE AND THE BOLD #60)

October: The evil Communist **Egg Fu the First** is introduced, meeting his demise the following month when his shell cracks under the force of Wonder Woman's golden lasso! (WONDER WOMAN #157)

1966

February: Wonder Girl and her boy buddies in the Teen Titans graduate to their own comic-book series (TEEN TITANS #1)

October: Wonder Woman meets **Horace Throstle,** a two-dimensional criminal known as **The Paper-Man!** (WONDER WOMAN #165)

November: Diana battles and destroys **Egg Fu the Fifth!** Strangely, she never encounters the second, third, or fourth Egg Fus. (WONDER WOMAN #166)

1967

April: The multi-limbed criminal **Crimson Centipede** makes his first and last appearance to date. (WONDER WOMAN #169)

May: Proving that the Amazing Amazon isn't the exception to DC Comics' belief that apes on covers sell more comics, a spacesuit-clad simian makes a monkey out of Diana in "Wonder Woman—Gorilla!" (WONDER WOMAN #170)

July–August: The Amazing Amazon is netted by the bizarre **Man-Fish** and held prisoner in his aquarium full of mermaids! (WONDER WOMAN #171)

1968

July: Wonder Woman first teams with Batman in the pages of THE BRAVE AND THE BOLD #78, this time to counter the threat of **Copperhead,** a contortionist assassin with a snakelike costume and poisonous fangs!

July–August: "For the honor of marrying **Klamos**" Wonder Woman is forced into a duel to the death with guest-star **Supergirl!** (WONDER WOMAN #177)

Unfortunately, young Diana had even less luck with love-struck boys tugging for her attention!

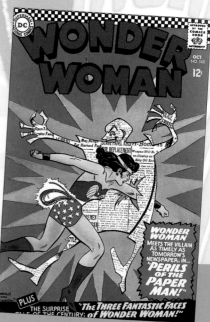

Read all about it! After falling into paper-making chemicals, Horace Throstle turned into a two-dimensional terror known as the Paper-Man!

When the Amazons journeyed to another dimension to renew their powers, Diana had to relinquish her costume and abilities. She updated her image and became a globetrotting adventuress!

September–October: A bold new direction for Wonder Woman begins as Diana forsakes her powers and costume. The incredible martial arts master **I-Ching** is introduced as Diana's new mentor. (WONDER WOMAN #178)

November–December: Diana's soon-to-be facially disfigured foe **Doctor Cyber** first appears. (WONDER WOMAN #179)

1969
January–February: Diana mourns the tragic death of her true love Steve Trevor and also meets private investigator **Tim Trench**. (WONDER WOMAN #180)

February: Wonder Woman resigns from JLA membership. (JUSTICE LEAGUE OF AMERICA #69)

August: Donna Troy's origins as Wonder Girl are revealed in the pages of TEEN TITANS #22.

1970
January: Wonder Woman teams up once again with Batman; however this time she does so without her Amazon powers. (THE BRAVE AND THE BOLD #87)

January–February: Diana meets **Morgana** the witch! (WONDER WOMAN #186)

1971
June: Diana faces the prospect of a shotgun wedding in a foreign land when she's asked if she'd rather be "a dead Diana Prince—or a live Queen?" on this issue's matrimonially-themed cover! (WONDER WOMAN #194)

Always a bride, but never a bridesmaid: Wonder Woman fended off a royal wedding as she continued to thwart tyrants of every stripe as plainclothes Diana Prince!

1972
May–June: Diana marks the 200th issue of WONDER WOMAN by battling her nemesis Doctor Cyber in "The Beauty Hater!"

July–August: Miaow!—the fur starts to fly as Diana first tussles with a different feline fatale, Batman's favorite arch-foe Catwoman! (WONDER WOMAN #201)

Who could possibly defeat Wonder Woman in gladiatorial combat on Paradise Island except… her own sister?! In WONDER WOMAN #204, Diana learned she wasn't the only child of clay given life by the gods! In the Amazon arena, Diana's family reunion with her sister Nubia almost became a family funeral!

September–October: Far away, in a land beyond time, sword and sorcery clash when Diana meets **Fafhrd the Barbarian** and the **Gray Mouser**. (WONDER WOMAN #202)

1973
January–February: Wonder Woman once more puts on her familiar star-spangled costume in time to meet her long-lost sister **Nubia**, another daughter that Queen Hippolyta molded from clay! Unfortunately, I-Ching dies in this issue! (WONDER WOMAN #204)

February: It's high time for another teaming of the Amazing Amazon with Gotham City's Caped Crusader in THE BRAVE AND THE BOLD #105!

For ten monthly issues, each Wonder Woman tale was narrated by one of her JLA teammates!

1974

June–July: Members of the Justice League of America begin appearing on the covers of the next ten issues of WONDER WOMAN as individual heroes introduce and recount their favorite adventures of the Amazing Amazon. Beginning with Superman, the line-up includes (in order): The Flash, Green Lantern, Aquaman, Black Canary, Green Arrow, Red Tornado and The Phantom Stranger, Elongated Man, The Atom, Hawkman, and Batman. (WONDER WOMAN #212)

1975

April–May: **The Duke of Deception** returns, using his powers to create illusions to bring about war! (WONDER WOMAN #217)

1976

January–February: It's a literal face-off for Wonder Woman when she's captured by vengeful Doctor Cyber, who plans to surgically remove Diana's beautiful face to replace her own hideously scarred visage! (WONDER WOMAN #221)

March: Wonder Woman rejoins the Justice League! (JUSTICE LEAGUE OF AMERICA #128)

April–May: By the grace of Aphrodite, Steve Trevor returns from the dead, animating a statue of himself as Steve Trevor Howard and learning Wonder Woman's secret identity. (WONDER WOMAN #223)

November–December: Diana first fights **Hephaestus the Fire-God**! (WONDER WOMAN #226)

December: Wonder Woman and Batman join together once more to thwart Catwoman. (THE BRAVE AND THE BOLD #130)

1977

January–February: The fiendish Nazi genius **Red Panzer** is introduced. (WONDER WOMAN #228)

May–June: Wonder Woman meets the evil **Osira**, an Egyptian sorceress freed from centuries of mummified slumber when an Axis tank inadvertently blasts her pyramid tomb! (WONDER WOMAN #231)

August–September: Wonder Woman battles a new Nazi nemesis: **Baron Blitzkrieg**! (WORLD'S FINEST COMICS #246)

Also this month, she meets **Armageddon**, yet another Axis agent determined to destroy Diana! (WONDER WOMAN #234)

November: The animorphing Japanese assassin **Kung** first appears. (WONDER WOMAN #237)

Diana's exploits during the 1970s included all-new adventures taking place during World War II and starring the Wonder Woman of Earth-2!

1978

March: Wonder Woman battles Adolf Hitler and the Nazis in DC SPECIAL SERIES #9, an 80-Page WONDER WOMAN SPECTACULAR comic.

Also this month, Diana shares billing with Batman yet again in THE BRAVE AND THE BOLD #140.

September: Wonder Woman meets the insidious **Inversion**, the Inside-Out Man! Also, this issue marks the beginning of TALES OF THE AMAZONS, a short-lived back-up feature chronicling the adventures of Diana's sisters in the ancient world. (WONDER WOMAN #247)

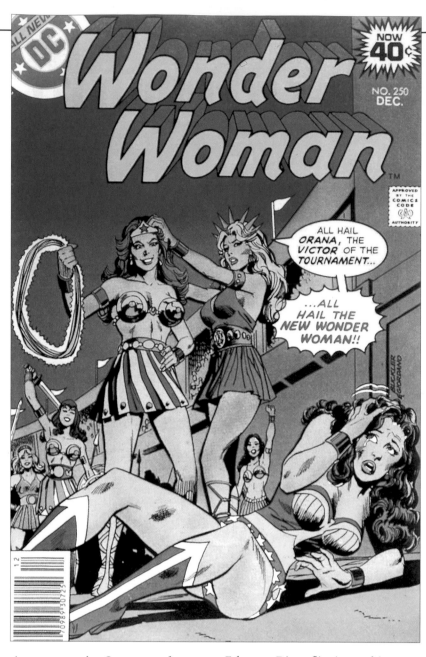

Amazon warrior Orana may have defeated Diana in the contest to select a new Wonder Woman, but her costumed career was tragically cut short.

October: Steve Trevor Howard dies again as Wonder Woman battles **The Dark Commander**! (WONDER WOMAN #248)

December: Diana experiences further sorrow in WONDER WOMAN #250 when she loses the mantle of Wonder Woman to her fellow Amazon warrior **Orana**!

Elsewhere, in the tabloid-sized SUPERMAN VS. WONDER WOMAN, the World War II-era Man of Steel and Diana clash over the use of the atomic bomb!

1979

January: "New" Wonder Woman Orana dies in combat with the evil **Warhead**. Diana once more takes up her lasso and bracelets to fulfill her destiny as the Amazing Amazon. (WONDER WOMAN #251)

February: Diana flies into orbit to save Skylab and an American space shuttle from **Astarte**, the Empress of the Silver Snake! Also, **Stacy Macklin** debuts as a fellow U. S. astronaut trainee alongside Diana Prince. (WONDER WOMAN #252)

March: Wonder Woman joins forces with the Man of Steel in Superman's fledgling team-up title, DC COMICS PRESENTS #9.

1980

January: Forget Steve Trevor! Wonder Woman meets a self-professed "real man," a desperado known as **The Gaucho**! (WONDER WOMAN #263)

Elsewhere, Wonder Woman teams with Batman for the last time in the pages of THE BRAVE AND THE BOLD. (THE BRAVE AND THE BOLD #158)

May: Wonder Woman begins a two-part team-up with Buddy Baker, the astounding **Animal Man**! (WONDER WOMAN #267)

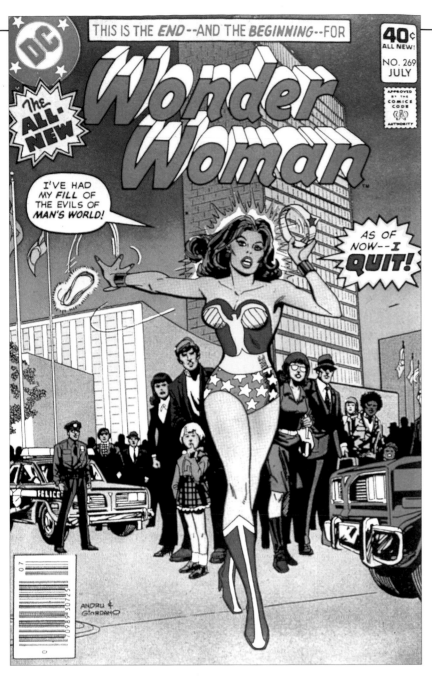

possessor of hypnotic and gravitational superpowers.

February: In a three-part arc beginning this issue, Wonder Woman finds herself wrapped in the coils of international terrorist **Kobra**, revealed here as the mastermind behind Deborah Domaine's transformation into Cheetah. (WONDER WOMAN #276)

April: Diana teams with Superman once again. (DC COMICS PRESENTS #32)

August: Wonder Woman teams with the **Demon Etrigan** to battle a Minotaur. (WONDER WOMAN #282)

September: The Greek gods' progenitors, the twelve Titans of Myth—**Cronus, Rhea, Iapetus, Themis, Hyperion, Thia, Crius, Mnemosyne, Oceanus, Tethys, Coeus,** and **Phoebe**—are introduced in the pages of THE NEW TEEN TITANS #11.

Also this month, Wonder Woman clashes with the **Red Dragon**, a Chinese counter-revolutionary rebel and warlord determined to return Communist China to a feudal system of rule (WONDER WOMAN #283)

1982
January: Wonder Woman teams with her adopted sister Wonder Girl and the New Teen Titans to thwart Dr. Cyber! (WONDER WOMAN #287)

Elsewhere this month, Wonder Woman returns to the pages of DC COMICS PRESENTS for another guest appearance. (DC COMICS PRESENTS #41)

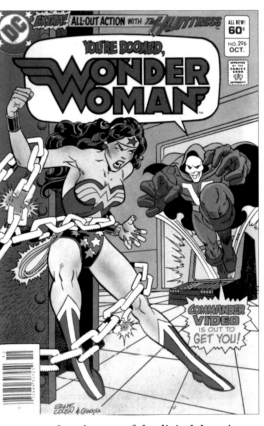

Leaping out of the digital domain, Commander Video—a creation of the mad genius General Electric—tried to kill a comic-book star!

February: **The Silver Swan** first appears as the Wonder Woman Foundation is introduced and the Amazing Amazon trades her eagle-emblem for the current WW-insignia in this groundbreaking issue. (WONDER WOMAN #288)

March: Dr. Psycho makes his first modern-day appearance in the guise of the less-than-heroic he-man **Captain Wonder**! (WONDER WOMAN #289)

October: In a nod to the growing popularity of electronic arcade games, Wonder Woman battles the evil **Commander Video**. (WONDER WOMAN #296)

November: Diana grapples with **Aegeus** (Greek terrorist **Nikos**), rider of winged Pegasus and hurler of magical thunderbolts! (WONDER WOMAN #297)

Fortunately, Diana's decision to quit the role of Wonder Woman was short-lived. After a spell of soul-searching on Paradise Island (lasting several issues), she was soon back in action!

July: As the classic cover of WONDER WOMAN #269 depicts, Diana briefly gives up the role of Wonder Woman and returns to Paradise Island when the problems of trying to keep the peace in man's world prove too much to bear. But there's another reason for Diana's return: she just can't forget her deceased paramour Steve Trevor!

August: Once more, as if answering Diana's prayers to Aphrodite, Steve Trevor returns from the dead. (WONDER WOMAN #270)

November: Wonder Girl joins Robin, Kid Flash, Changeling, and newcomers Raven, Cyborg, and Starfire to form a **New Teen Titans**! (THE NEW TEEN TITANS #1)

September: Wonder Woman's origin is retold… again! Also this issue, Earth-2's **The Huntress** (daughter of that parallel world's Batman and Catwoman) begins a long-running stint as an 8-page back-up feature in this title. (WONDER WOMAN #271)

Once more, Diana proved that of all the Amazons on Paradise Island, she alone was worthiest of the costume and the mantle of Wonder Woman!

December: Debutante **Deborah Domaine** turns to crime and becomes a second Cheetah! (WONDER WOMAN #274)

1981
January: In WORLD'S FINEST #266, Stacy Macklin is bathed in the rays of strange radiation and assumes the split personality of **Lady Lunar,** the

In WONDER WOMAN #300, Diana learned that Dr. Garrett Sanford, the sleep dust-sprinkling Sandman, only had eyes for her!

1983

February: It's super-hero guest-stars galore in the celebratory 300th issue of WONDER WOMAN! Hippolyta "Lyta" Trevor—a.k.a. **Fury**—debuts in this issue as daughter of the Earth-2 Wonder Woman and General Steve Trevor.

July: Diana first encounters the scheming enchantress **Circe** in modern continuity. (WONDER WOMAN #305)

1984

January: **Dick Grayson**, a.k.a. **Robin the Teen Wonder**, investigates Donna Troy's parentage and true origins in "Who Is Donna Troy?" At story's end, Donna is reunited with her adoptive parents. (THE NEW TEEN TITANS #39)

April: The Amazon Princess adds another god to her Rogues Gallery, the Aztec jaguar lord **Tezcatlipoca**! (WONDER WOMAN #314)

May: Tezcatlipoca's mind-bending Hall of Mirrors reveals Diana Prince's world-famous alter ego to this Aztec adversary! (WONDER WOMAN #315)

December: Wonder Woman makes her final guest appearance teaming with Superman in DC COMICS PRESENTS #76.

1985

February: As the cover to this issue declares, Etta Candy assumes the role and powers of Wonder Woman for one night only to thwart the

combined might of Doctor Psycho (as Wonder Man), Cheetah, Angle Man, and the Silver Swan! (WONDER WOMAN #323)

Etta Candy learned the hard way that it's not so easy being Wonder Woman when she spent a whole night in possession of Diana's powers and costume!

April: DC Comics' 12-issue, world-rending miniseries CRISIS ON INFINITE EARTHS begins this month, erasing Earth-2 and other parallel universes from continuity. By story's end, a single unified Earth will emerge, while the company's substantial stable of characters will find their origins and histories significantly revised.

Also this month, the new **Atomic Knight** debuts as an armed forces ally to Wonder Woman. (WONDER WOMAN #324)

1986

February: To make way for the Amazing Amazon's post-CRISIS revamp, WONDER WOMAN ends its long and uninterrupted publication run at issue #329. Though the story is soon wiped from continuity, Diana finally marries Steve Trevor.

March: As the CRISIS draws to a close, Diana is returned to clay, thus setting the stage for one of DC Comics' most successful relaunches. (CRISIS ON INFINITE EARTHS #12)

May: The Amazing Amazon's "Golden Age" is revisited in DC's four-issue THE LEGEND OF WONDER WOMAN miniseries, beginning this month.

1987

February: Princess Diana of Themyscira returns to comics with a new origin, a new mission, and a new DC Comics series written and illustrated by George Pérez and Greg Potter! The Greek war-god **Ares** first appears here, as does Diana's mother **Hippolyta**. As well, both the "Lion of Olympus" **Heracles** and **Steve Trevor** are reintroduced. (WONDER WOMAN vol. 2 #1)

March: **Etta Candy**, this time a career Air Force officer and aide to Trevor, returns to continuity. The demonic **Decay** and Ares' children **Deimos** (God of Terror), **Phobos** (God of

THE LEGEND OF WONDER WOMAN miniseries bridged the gap between Diana's return to clay in DC's epic CRISIS ON INFINITE EARTHS and her rebirth in an all-new, ongoing series!

Fear), and **Harmonia** (Goddess of Balance) first appear. Also, Hestia's golden Lasso of Truth is forged here. (WONDER WOMAN vol. 2 #2)

Also this month, the "Golden Age" Fury's origins are chronicled in SECRET ORIGINS vol. 2 #12.

April: **Professor Julia Kapatelis**— Diana's mentor and surrogate mother in "Patriarch's World"—and her daughter **Vanessa "Nessie" Kapatelis** first appear. (WONDER WOMAN vol. 2 #3)

Also this month, Wonder Woman is introduced to the general public. (LEGENDS #6)

June: In battle with Deimos, Diana beheads this monstrous son of Ares with a single throw of her razor-sharp royal tiara. (WONDER WOMAN vol. 2 #5)

In just 32 pages, DC Comics relaunched Wonder Woman with a brand-new first issue chronicling over 30 millennia of Amazon history, beginning with Hippolyta's origins as a murdered cavewoman, the Olympian gods' creation of the Amazon sisterhood and its betrayal by Heracles, Diana's creation from Themysciran clay, and her eventual triumph in the contest to become Wonder Woman!

Also this month, Fury joins up with the Axis-busting **Young All-Stars** during World War II. (YOUNG ALL-STARS #1)

July: Wonder Woman prevents Ares from annihilating the Earth in nuclear fire! (WONDER WOMAN *vol. 2 #6*)

Diana was not born just to provide Hippolyta with a long-awaited child. The Greek gods of Olympus also created her to oppose the destructive drives of the god of war, Ares, and promote peace on Earth.

August: Archaeologist and stop-at-nothing treasure hunter **Barbara Minerva** first appears, alongside Diana's future publicist, the troubled media mogul **Myndi Mayer**. (WONDER WOMAN *vol. 2 #7*)

October: Urzkatargan native priest **Chuma** reveals the secret ancient ritual that transforms Barbara Minerva into **The Cheetah**! (WONDER WOMAN *vol. 2 #9*)

November: Diana enters Doom's Doorway on Themyscira, the entrance to Pandora's Box! (WONDER WOMAN *vol. 2 #10*)

December: Diana's warrior namesake, **Diana Rockwell Trevor**, appears. (WONDER WOMAN *vol. 2 #11*)

By slaying the monstrous and many-armed Cottus, Diana Rockwell Trevor gave her life so that the Amazons could live.

1988

January: Diana learns the story of Diana Rockwell Trevor, Steve Trevor's mother and her namesake. (WONDER WOMAN *vol. 2* #12)

February: In the netherworld beneath Doom's Doorway, Wonder Woman and Hippolyta battle the monsters **Cyclops**, **Minotaur**, and **Echidna**! (WONDER WOMAN *vol. 2* #13)

Publicist Myndi Mayer did much to improve Wonder Woman's image in Patriarch's World. But Mayer was haunted by her own demons...

March: The Amazons forgive Heracles for his betrayal and enslavement of their kind. (WONDER WOMAN *vol. 2* #14)

April: **Valerie Beaudry**, a.k.a. **The Silver Swan**, is reintroduced in a tale also featuring the debut of Boston police inspector **Ed Indelicato**, who soon develops a crush on the Amazing Amazon. (WONDER WOMAN *vol. 2* #15)

May: Wonder Woman and Superman share a tentative kiss during a date in ACTION COMICS #600, which also features Diana's first encounter with world-conquering tyrant **Darkseid**, who destroys Mount Olympus!

June: **Circe** returns as a vengeful sorceress capable of transforming men into terrible were-creatures! (WONDER WOMAN *vol. 2* #17)

July: **Cronus**, father of the Greek gods, first appears as a gnarled and dead tree in the darkness of Hades. Also, this issue includes the first 16-page LEGENDS OF THE AMAZONS bonus comic feature. (WONDER WOMAN *vol. 2* #18)

August: The powerful witch **Hecate** gives her soul to Circe. (WONDER WOMAN *vol. 2* #19)

September: In "Who Killed Myndi Mayer?" Diana investigates the suspected murder of her troubled publicist, later revealed to have died from a drug overdose. (WONDER WOMAN *vol. 2* #20)

October: The Greek gods resolve to leave the ruins of Mount Olympus behind and embark on a great Cosmic Migration. (WONDER WOMAN *vol. 2* #21)

November: The Amazons vote to open up Themyscira to the outside world for the first time and allow men to set foot on their sacred Paradise Island. (WONDER WOMAN *vol. 2* #22)

December: Wonder Woman struggles to subdue **Ixion**, Earth's first mass murderer, after the beast is loosed from its imprisonment in Tartarus. (WONDER WOMAN *vol. 2* #23-24)

Also this year, the first ever WONDER WOMAN ANNUAL is published, featuring a tale of Diana's childhood on Themyscira. It is revealed here that Julia Kapatelis was raised from infancy on Themyscira. (WONDER WOMAN ANNUAL #1)

1989

January: WONDER WOMAN *vol. 2* #26 includes the second 16-page bonus LEGENDS OF THE AMAZONS comic feature.

February: The Cheetah steals the Lasso of Truth, forcing Diana to battle without her famed lariat for several months while in search of it. (WONDER WOMAN *vol. 2* #27)

April: **The Bana-Mighdall**, so-called "Lost Tribe of Amazons," is introduced. (WONDER WOMAN *vol. 2* #29)

Elsewhere this month, Wonder Woman joins the Justice League on a part-time basis. (JUSTICE LEAGUE EUROPE #1)

June: Donna Troy, once the original Wonder Girl, adopts a new costume and superheroic identity: **Troia**! (THE NEW TITANS #55)

September: Wonder Woman first meets and battles **Shim'Tar**, chief warrior of the Bana-Mighdall. (WONDER WOMAN *vol. 2* #34)

October: After many centuries, Hippolyta's golden girdle is returned to her by Diana, who also reclaims Hestia's Lasso. (WONDER WOMAN *vol. 2* #35)

December: Ares's daughter **Eris** (Goddess of Strife) is introduced as twelve United Nations delegates (some of them men) are permitted to visit Themyscira. (WONDER WOMAN *vol. 2* #37)

Also this year, WONDER WOMAN ANNUAL #2 features the Amazing Amazon as rendered by an all-female roster of comic book artists.

1990

June: Beginning with this issue, Diana learns about the tragic past of the Silver Swan. (WONDER WOMAN *vol. 2* #43)

August: The legacy of Pandora's Box is revealed in a tale that foretells Diana's death and the means by which she is resurrected during the

WONDER WOMAN ANNUAL #1 revealed the secrets of Doom's Doorway and the horrors locked behind it as Julia and Vanessa Kapatelis first visited Themyscira.

forthcoming WAR OF THE GODS. (WONDER WOMAN *vol. 2* #45)

October: Vanessa Kapatelis's best friend **Lucy Spears** commits suicide. Vanessa's anguish over Lucy's death will, years later, contribute to her unwitting transformation into the supervillain Silver Swan! (WONDER WOMAN *vol. 2* #46)

November: Wonder Woman and Troia finally meet! (WONDER WOMAN vol. 2 #47)

1991

January: WONDER WOMAN marks its milestone 50th issue with Queen Hippolyta's journey to a United Nations ceremony to officially open Themysciran relations with the nations of Earth and reunite the Amazons with Patriarch's World.

May: Mind-meddler **Doctor Psycho** is reintroduced as the murderer and impersonator of psychologist **Dr. Charles Stanton**. (WONDER WOMAN *vol. 2* #54)

June: Vanessa Kapatelis is first used as an unwilling pawn in Dr. Psycho's mind games against Wonder Woman. (WONDER WOMAN *vol. 2* #55)

During the WAR OF THE GODS, Heracles saved Themyscira by taking up Atlas's burden and carrying the weight of the world on his shoulders!

September: WAR OF THE GODS begins! DC Comics' epic four-issue miniseries and sweeping inter-company crossover finds Diana teaming with scores of heroes and heroines when Circe incites conflict among many pantheons of gods in her scheme to rend asunder Gaea herself. (WAR OF THE GODS #1)

November: Hermes is killed by Circe. And, apparently, so is Diana when Circe reverts the Amazing Amazon to clay! (WAR OF THE GODS #3)

Elsewhere this month, as the WAR OF THE GODS rages on, Wonder Woman battles the intergalactic bounty hunter and malcontent known as **Lobo**! (WONDER WOMAN *vol. 2* #60)

1992
January: In "To Avenge an Amazon," Diana is mourned by her friends and family and heroic comrades. (WONDER WOMAN *vol. 2* #61)

Elsewhere, Diana is reborn when Hippolyta re-molds her body from the ashes of Diana's funeral pyre which burned with the fire of Pandora. The resurrected Wonder Woman defeats Circe and ends her apocalyptic conflict. (WAR OF THE GODS #4)

February: WONDER WOMAN #62 marks the departure of writer, plotter, and artist George Pérez, who had chronicled the Amazing Amazon's adventures since the title's

relaunch in 1986. The title undergoes a brief, four-month hiatus. In this issue, Diana helps to celebrate Vanessa Kapatelis's graduation from junior high school.

June: Wonder Woman returns to monthly status in WONDER WOMAN #63, continuing a story begun in this month's WONDER WOMAN SPECIAL #1, featuring Diana joining forces with **Deathstroke the Terminator** to free Barbara Minerva from the Muldavian monarch **Daemonstro** and his monstrous servant **Drax**.

August: Doctor Psycho makes Vanessa Kapatelis the target of another psychic assault. (WONDER WOMAN *vol. 2* #65)

September: Wonder Woman joins Justice League Europe as a regular member. (JUSTICE LEAGUE EUROPE #42)

Also this month, Diana journeys into space in order to save a stranded Russian cosmonaut. Unfortunately, Diana and the cosmonaut, **Natasha Teranova**, are flung into deep space by **Thomas Asquith Randolph**, the hero-turned-villain known as **The White Magician**, introduced here. Diana and Natasha spend the next six issues battling intergalactic slavers and the dreaded **Sangtee Empire**! (WONDER WOMAN *vol. 2* #66)

December: Diana meets the Daxamite she comes to call "Julia," after Julia Kapatelis. Initially, the two are enemies. (WONDER WOMAN *vol. 2* #69)

Also this year, a roguish role-reversal takes place when Wonder Woman is "eclipsed" by the villain known as **Eclipso** and directly battles the White Magician for the first time! (WONDER WOMAN ANNUAL #3)

1993
March: After more than six months, Diana returns to Earth. (WONDER WOMAN *vol. 2* #72)

April: The Amazon Princess takes a job as a waitress at Taco Whiz! (WONDER WOMAN *vol. 2* #73)

August: The evil crime lord **Ares Buchanan** is introduced as the Greek war god Ares takes possession of the body of small-time criminal **Ari Buchanan**. (WONDER WOMAN *vol. 2* #77)

September: The drug-fueled high-velocity hitwoman **Mayfly** targets Diana for assassination! (WONDER WOMAN *vol. 2* #78)

November: Mayfly ends her brief life in a vain attempt to escape incarceration. (WONDER WOMAN *vol. 2* #80)

December: Diana meets Assistant D. A. **Donna Milton.** (WONDER WOMAN *vol. 2* #81)

1994
March: Adrift on stormy waters, Diana helps Donna Milton give birth to her infant daughter, the child of Ares! Also this issue, the White Magician murders mobster **Tony Sazia**, leaving **Julia Sazia** in control of his Boston criminal holdings. (WONDER WOMAN *vol. 2* #84)

June: Wonder Woman trades punches with the superpowered criminals known as **Rockface** and **Plaasma**! (WONDER WOMAN vol. 2 #87)

August: Following the loss of her godlike powers, Donna Troy joins the **Darkstars**, maser-wielding, peacekeepers, empowered by the enigmatic **Controllers**. Donna's stay with the Darkstars is brief. (THE DARKSTARS #23)

In the second contest to choose an Amazon fit to be Wonder Woman, Diana battled terrifying monsters of myth as well as human forces conspiring against her!

September: Dissatisfied with Diana's performance as Wonder Woman, Queen Hippolyta calls for a new contest to decide Themyscira's Amazon representative to Patriarch's World. (WONDER WOMAN *vol. 2* #90)

October: Wonder Woman briefly assumes the leadership of **Justice League America**, commanding a team that includes The Flash, Metamorpho, Crimson Fox, Fire, Nuklon, Obsidian, and Hawkman. (JUSTICE LEAGUE AMERICA #0)

November: The Amazon **Artemis** of the Bana-Mighdall tribe first appears. (WONDER WOMAN *vol. 2* #90)

December: Artemis wins the contest while Diana is preoccupied with saving her fellow competitors from jeopardy! (WONDER WOMAN *vol. 2* #90)

Diana soon discovered that serving fast food wasn't quite as fulfilling as fighting for world peace!

Diana showed Artemis and the world that there was room enough for two Amazing Amazons!

1995
January: Artemis assumes the role of Wonder Woman. Diana also continues to operate as Wonder Woman, but in a different costume. (WONDER WOMAN *vol. 2* #93).

February: Diana takes on the triple-threat of the assassin known as **Cheshire**, The Cheetah, and Batman's fetching foe **Poison Ivy**! (WONDER WOMAN *vol. 2* #94)

March: The Cheetah actually saves Diana's life, preventing Cheshire from stabbing Wonder Woman in the back! (WONDER WOMAN *vol. 2* #95)

April: Wonder Woman confronts Batman's greatest enemy, **The Joker**! (WONDER WOMAN *vol. 2* #96)

The Clown Prince of Crime did his level best to make sure that Diana died laughing!

Early July: The White Magician forsakes his humanity to become a horned **High Lord Daemon**, offering up both his lover **Cassie Arnold** and The Cheetah as sacrifices to his unholy brethren. The Cheetah's demise may be premature, however. (WONDER WOMAN vol. 2 #99)

July: As Artemis perishes in battle with The White Magician, Diana reclaims the mantle of Wonder Woman in the centennial WONDER WOMAN *vol. 2* #100, which also includes the revelation that Circe is now mother to an infant daughter conceived by Ares when the sorceress masqueraded as Donna Milton!

August: Diana meets police officer **Mike Schorr** when she relocates to Northern California's Gateway City. Also beginning here, Darkseid brings ruin to Themyscira in a conflict that results in the slaughter of nearly half the Amazons! (WONDER WOMAN *vol. 2* #101)

November: **Neron** is introduced as quite possibly the devil himself in DC Comics' UNDERWORLD UNLEASHED crossover event, which chronicles the demon lord's attempts to corrupt the incorruptible souls of super heroes after augmenting the powers of their supervillain foes. (UNDERWORLD UNLEASHED #1)

Also this year, the "Year One" themed WONDER WOMAN ANNUAL #4 chronicles a spectacular bygone battle between Diana and The Cheetah!

1996
February: Gateway City Museum curator **Helena Sandsmark** and her daughter **Cassandra "Cassie" Sandsmark** first appear. (WONDER WOMAN *vol. 2* #105)

March: Beginning this issue, Wonder Woman teams with the demon Etrigan and the Phantom Stranger to battle the Medieval sorceress **Morgaine Le Fay**. (WONDER WOMAN *vol. 2* #107)

May: Heracles returns disguised as the heroic **Harold Campion** (a.k.a. **Champion**) in a plot to seduce and have revenge on Diana. Beginning this issue, Wonder Woman battles virtual clones of friends and foes (including the late Flash Barry Allen and Green Lantern Hal Jordan's deceased foe Sinestro) created by the Virtual Reanimator, an invention of

Dr. Julian Lazarus (a.k.a **The Death Doctor**) to keep the consciousness of his own dead son alive! (WONDER WOMAN *vol. 2* #109)

June: Artemis returns from the dead in ARTEMIS: REQUIEM, a six-issue miniseries that includes the Amazon warrior's ill-fated marriage to the demon **Dalkriig-Hath** and the introduction of supernatural hunters **The Hellenders**. (ARTEMIS: REQUIEM #1)

July: Cassie Sandsmark becomes the new costumed **Wonder Girl** by donning the Sandals of Hermes and the Gauntlet of Atlas… just in time to battle a virtual clone of Decay! (WONDER WOMAN *vol. 2* #111)

In thrall to sorceress Morgaine Le Fay, the demon Etrigan was dispatched to capture Wonder Woman so that Le Fay could steal Diana's immortality. But Diana was no longer immortal!

August: Diana destroys a virtual clone of the alien monster who killed Superman: **Doomsday**! Also, Mike Schorr puts a stop to the Death Doctor's Virtual Reanimator. (WONDER WOMAN *vol. 2* #112)

October: Doctor Psycho mentally manipulates Vanessa Kapatelis yet again, a psychic attack with a lingering impact on the troubled teen. Also this issue, Diana learns that she is reverting to the clay from which she was molded! (WONDER WOMAN *vol. 2* #114)

November: The otherworldly vehicle which will become Wonder Woman's Invisible Jet first appears. Also, Champion steals a kiss from a stunned Diana! (WONDER WOMAN *vol. 2* #115)

December: The blind alien **Lansinarians** are introduced. (WONDER WOMAN *vol. 2* #116)

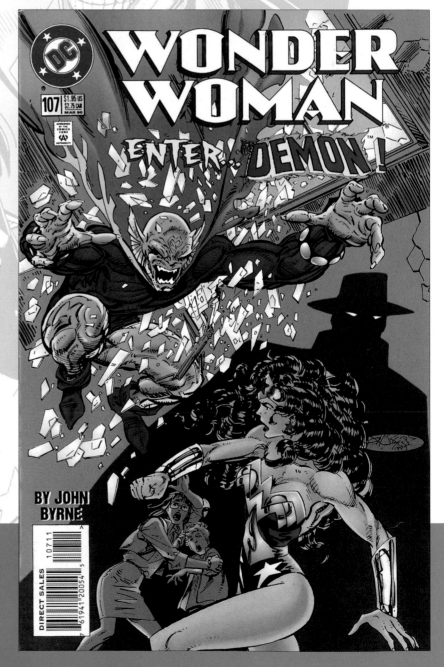

This year's WONDER WOMAN ANNUAL #6 tells one of the "Legends of the Dead Earth," in which a young woman called **AlyXa** finds peace between her **Unremembered** tribe and the horrifically transformed **Ratbats** when she meets a female Ratbat clad as Wonder Woman!

Also, DC Comics releases its groundbreaking, four-issue miniseries KINGDOM COME, an epic "Elseworlds" tale of a near-future in which Wonder Woman finds herself at odds with Superman and Batman on the difficult task of reining in the roguish superpowered progeny of a past generation of heroes. By the end of the story, order has been restored and Diana reveals to a not-so-surprised Bruce Wayne that she and Clark Kent are expecting a super-baby!

1997
January: WONDER WOMAN PLUS… #1 features Diana's first teaming with super-speedy siren **Jesse Quick**!

Also this month, Wonder Woman joins fellow heavy-hitters Superman, Batman, Flash, Aquaman, Green Lantern, and Martian Manhunter to form an all-new **Justice League of America**, with headquarters on the Moon. (JLA #1)

Elsewhere, Wonder Girl joins the teen team known as **Young Justice**! (YOUNG JUSTICE #4)

And in the pages of WONDER WOMAN *vol. 2* #117, the Lansinarians bequeath Diana her Invisible Jet!

February: In battle with a maddened and mindless Cheetah, Diana loses a brittle clay hand! (WONDER WOMAN *vol. 2* #118)

March: Her hand restored, Diana successfully frees Barbara Minerva from her Cheetah form. (WONDER WOMAN *vol. 2* #119)

April: WONDER WOMAN celebrates its 10th anniversary issue! (WONDER WOMAN *vol. 2* #120)

May: Diana and the Amazons are transformed into stone statues, while Diana's petrified body shatters after striking Champion (a.k.a. Heracles)! (WONDER WOMAN *vol. 2* #121)

June: Heracles beseeches his father Zeus to spare Diana and her Amazon sisters. After restoring the Amazons to life, Zeus grants Cassie Sandsmark her "fondest wish," bequeathing her superpowers of her very own. (WONDER WOMAN *vol. 2* #122)

revive her—but in vain! (WONDER WOMAN *vol. 2* #125)

October: DC Comics' ADVENTURE COMICS 80-PAGE GIANT #1 purports to chronicle Hippolyta's final battle with the wandering evil spirit **Dark Angel** in 1950, when she teamed with fellow JSA member Johnny Thunder to send the evil spirit into infinite exile. Unfortunately, Dark Angel will return to menace Hippolyta's daughters in the present-day.

July: Diana and Artemis battle the demon Etrigan! (WONDER WOMAN *vol. 2* #123)

August: Great Hera! The demon Neron succeeds in slaying Diana! (WONDER WOMAN *vol. 2* #124)

September: **Dr. Doris Zeul**, the scientist who will later become **Giganta**, first appears as Diana's compatriots in the JLA attempt to

As she once again reverted to the clay that formed her, Diana relived the most significant episodes of her life in this milestone issue of WONDER WOMAN!

This story saw the restoration of Mount Olympus and Heracles professing his love for Diana!

Also this month, Hippolyta's physical abilities are enhanced when she encounters **The Source**! (WONDER WOMAN *vol. 2* #126)

November: Diana becomes **Goddess of Truth** on Olympus. (WONDER WOMAN *vol. 2* #127)

December: On Earth, Hippolyta assumes the role of Wonder Woman, and **Egg Fu** returns as a computerized creation of Darkseid! (WONDER WOMAN *vol. 2* #128)

1998

March: Untold secrets of Diana and her origins are revealed in DC Comics' WONDER WOMAN SECRET FILES #1.

Also this month, Dark Angel is summoned by Baroness Paula Von Gunther to attack Hippolyta and the Justice Society of America during World War II! (WONDER WOMAN vol. 2 #131)

June: During DC Comics' GIRLFRENZY story event, Donna Troy appears in her own one-shot issue in which she battles **Red Panzer**. (WONDER WOMAN: DONNA TROY)

Elsewhere, "Who Is Donna Troy?" reveals that Donna is actually a creation of Dark Angel! (WONDER WOMAN vol. 2 #134)

August: Diana returns from Olympus and resumes her duties as Wonder Woman, using her golden lasso to turn the Flash's memories of Donna Troy into truth, thereby restoring Donna's own unique identity. Also in this issue, the intellect of a dying Dr. Zeul is transferred into the gorilla body of **Giganta**! (WONDER WOMAN vol. 2 #136)

September: Myndi Mayer's ghost implores Diana from beyond the grave to save her sister **Wendy** from the terrible drug known as Lethe in a tale featuring the return of Ed Indelicato. (WONDER WOMAN ANNUAL #7)

In this bittersweet WONDER WOMAN ANNUAL, Detective Ed Indelicato overcame his unrequited feelings for Diana and found new love with Wendy Mayer.

Also this month, Queen Hippolyta awakens to find herself a suburban wife and mother in a dreamworld created by Circe! (WONDER WOMAN vol. 2 #137)

November: In the year 85,271, Wonder Woman and Artemis journey to the planet Venus, "terraformed" over many centuries to become the new home of the Amazons! (WONDER WOMAN vol. 2 #1,000,000)

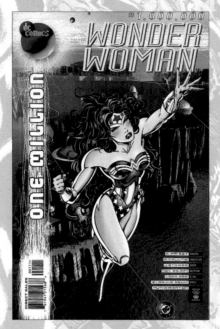

During DC's ONE MILLION crossover, today's heroes joined their 853rd century counterparts to defeat Vandal Savage and Solaris!

December: The 50-headed, 100-armed Titan—a monstrous child of Cronus—first appears. (WONDER WOMAN vol. 2 #139)

Elsewhere this year, WONDER WOMAN: THE ONCE AND FUTURE STORY finds Diana's translation of an ancient tablet's tale of ancient Greece eerily mirroring her present-day struggle to extricate an archaeologist friend from an abusive relationship.

This special story included facts about domestic violence and important phone numbers to call for victims seeking help from abuse.

1999

January: Wonder Woman first battles the monster of memory **Oblivion**, another of the Titan Cronus's horrific progeny! (WONDER WOMAN vol. 2 #140)

February: Donna Troy regains her Amazonian superpowers and returns to action as Troia! (JLA/TITANS #3)

Elsewhere, a base for Diana, the WonderDome, is created. (WONDER WOMAN vol. 2 #141)

March: **The Sphinx**, **Pegasus**, **Ladon**, and **Chiron**—all creatures of Greek myth—first appear and take up residence in a crystal garden within the WonderDome. At Diana's request, Artemis becomes Cassie Sandsmark's teacher in her training to master the skills necessary to be an officially sanctioned Wonder Girl. (WONDER WOMAN vol. 2 #142)

Also this month, Troia returns to active duty with the original lineup of Teen Titans in their adult incarnations. (THE TITANS #1)

April: As counterpoint to Diana, the mad Cronus creates the mayhem-making **Devastation** as a weapon to wage war against both god and man. (WONDER WOMAN vol. 2 #143)

June: Cronus is reborn with a new appearance as more of his children—**Harrier**, **Disdain**, and **Arch**—make their monstrous debuts. Cronus's cyclopean/centaurian brother **Slaughter** is introduced. (WONDER WOMAN vol. 2 #145)

July: Devastation's occult origins are chronicled in this month's WONDER WOMAN SECRET FILES #2.

August: Hippolyta returns to active duty alongside the Justice Society in the pages of DC Comics' new ongoing JSA #1.

Also this month, the GODWAR begins as Cronus and his terrible children storm Olympus and turn its gods and goddesses to stone in their bid to rule over all of creation! (WONDER WOMAN vol. 2 #147)

September: After receiving her education in Patriarch's World, **Akila** of the Bana-Mighdall assumes the mantle of Shim'Tar, using a techno-mystical battlesuit to help Wonder Woman and Artemis defeat the simian forces of gorilla queen Abu-Gita. Also this issue, **Nu'Bia** is reintroduced as an Amazon warrior chosen centuries ago to guard Doom's Doorway. (WONDER WOMAN ANNUAL #8)

Also this month, Diana meets the blue-skinned Hindu warrior avatar **Rama**, who falls in love with the Amazing Amazon! (WONDER WOMAN vol. 2 #148)

October: Diana first visits Mount Mandara, home of the Hindu

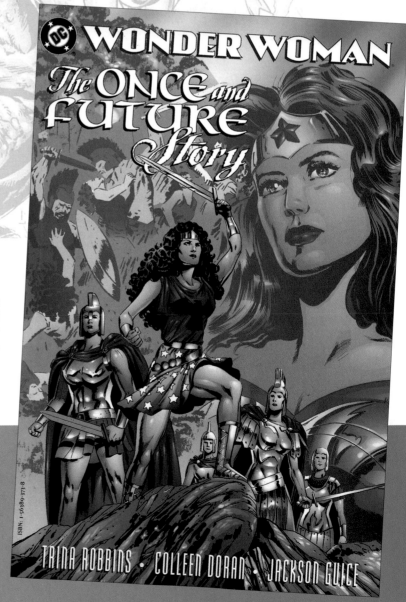

pantheon of gods. (WONDER WOMAN *vol. 2* #149)

November: WONDER WOMAN reaches its 150th issue as the Greek and Hindu gods prevent Cronus from usurping the throne of Heaven!

December: A new **Doctor Poison**, granddaughter of Princess Maru—the original Dr. Poison who battled Hippolyta's Wonder Woman during World War II—is introduced as the psychopathic genius behind the monster-making **Pandora Virus**. (WONDER WOMAN *vol. 2* #151)

2000
February: Wonder Girl takes center stage in an issue culminating with her first kiss from her biggest crush, Superboy! (WONDER WOMAN *vol. 2* #153)

March: Diana and Nu'Bia battle the metahuman terrorists **Doctor Echo** and **Blue Ice** when Nu'Bia journeys to Patriarch's World in order to recapture the demon-king **Ahriman**. Blue Ice dies here. (WONDER WOMAN *vol. 2* #154)

July: Cassie Sandsmark is brainwashed by Devastation into battling Wonder Woman! However, Cassie slips Deva's mental grip and defeats the child of Cronus. For her efforts, Cassie is made an honorary Amazon and is decreed worthy of the name Wonder Girl! (WONDER WOMAN *vol. 2* #158)

August: Diana establishes the WonderDome as her embassy in Patriarch's World and reestablishes the "Wonder Scouts," inactive since World War II. (WONDER WOMAN *vol. 2* #159)

September: Eager to steal her powers, Batman's foe **Clayface** sets his sights on the Amazon originally made of clay, Princess Diana of Themyscira! (WONDER WOMAN *vol. 2* #160)

November: Wonder Woman and Aquaman join forces to thwart the Atlantean monarch's nemesis **Black Manta** and his monstrous **Gorgomaids**! (WONDER WOMAN *vol. 2* #162)

Elsewhere this year, Wonder Woman has to betray her JLA teammates in order to save their lives when a prophesy spells their doom. (JLA: A LEAGUE OF ONE)

Diana goes it alone in JLA: A LEAGUE OF ONE. She must face the last dragon on Earth, an ancient menace that now threatens the modern world with primordial evil!

2001

January: As the four-part miniseries GODS OF GOTHAM begins, Wonder Woman and her super sisters join forces with the Dark Knight and his squires to save Gotham City from the terrifying children of Ares! (WONDER WOMAN *vol. 2* #164)

March: DC Comics' JUSTICE LEAGUES crossover features the one-shot JUSTICE LEAGUE OF AMAZONS starring Wonder Woman and a lineup of super heroines.

May: The Amazon Magala incites civil war on Themyscira, pitting the Amazons against their Bana-Mighdall sisters. Fury becomes Magala's unwitting pawn in a deadly power struggle to rule Paradise Island. (WONDER WOMAN *vol. 2* #168)

June: As the Amazonian civil war concludes with Magala's death at the hands of the avatar of Tisiphone, the power of Fury, Artemis takes up the role of Shim'Tar to lead the Bana-Mighdall Amazons. (WONDER WOMAN *vol. 2* #169)

July: Reporter **Lois Lane** follows a day in the life of Wonder Woman. Also, Diana meets United Nations Rural Development Organization (UNRDO) worker **Trevor Barnes**. Corporate raider **Sébastian Ballesteros** also first appears here, and a new **Silver Swan** makes a very brief cameo appearance. (WONDER WOMAN *vol. 2* #170)

August: Sébastian Ballesteros is transformed into the second **Cheetah** and in turn cybernetically alters Diana's young friend Vanessa

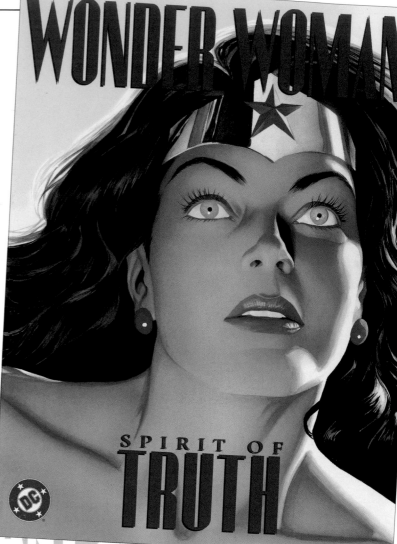

Kapatelis into the new Silver Swan! (WONDER WOMAN *vol. 2* #171)

September: Hippolyta valiantly perishes in battle with Imperiex, sacrificing her own life to save Diana's. The Daxamite Julia returns as an ally in the cataclysmic Imperiex War. (WONDER WOMAN *vol. 2* #172)

October: Themyscira is moved into outer space as a defensive line against the advancing probes of the world-destroying Imperiex. Unfortunately, the storied "Paradise Island" is destroyed! Also, in battle with Darkseid, Diana "corrupts" his evil soul with her innate goodness after funneling her spiritual energy into him. (WONDER WOMAN *vol. 2* #173)

In the special issue WONDER WOMAN: OUR WORLDS AT WAR #1, the legacy of Hippolyta is explored following her death. In an untold tale of

Broken and bleeding in Superman's arms, Wonder Woman was unable to save her mother Hippolyta from the terrible power of Imperiex.

Proceeds of the sale of art from SPIRIT OF TRUTH were donated to a charity benefiting the victims of the 9/11 terrorist attacks in the United States.

this "original" Amazing Amazon, **Villainy Inc.** is reintroduced as a criminal consortium assembled by the Atlantean **Queen Clea** to overrun her native Atlantis.

November: DC Comics publishes the tabloid-sized WONDER WOMAN: SPIRIT OF TRUTH, a collaboration between Emmy Award-winning animator Paul Dini and KINGDOM COME artist Alex Ross.

Also this month, Circe returns and transforms the male citizens of New York City into bestiamorphs while her army of lady supervillains takes over! Circe's daughter **Lyta** (after Hippolyta) appears here as a toddler. (WONDER WOMAN *vol. 2* #174)

2002

March: Greek, Egyptian, and other goddesses, patron deities of the Amazons and their sister Bana-Mighdall respectively, combine to forge a new Themyscira. Hippolyta's spirit is infused within the resurrected Paradise Island, now a

floating archipelago melded with the WonderDome's bio-technology. Also, Wonder Woman's Invisible Jet zooms back into action with a streamlined new design! (WONDER WOMAN *vol. 2 #177*)

April: Smooth-talking thief-for-hire **The Angle Man** (a.k.a. **Angelo Bend**) returns to continuity. He now possesses a triangular-shaped weapon capable of warping space. (WONDER WOMAN vol. 2 #178)

Diana's romantic evening with Trevor Barnes is rudely interrupted by a prehistoric sea creature, and they are whisked away to the savage world of Skartaris!

May: The sorceress **Jinx**, three-faced **Trinity**, scientist Doctor Poison, giantess Giganta, and **Cyborgirl** join the ranks of Villainy Inc. to aid Clea's invasion of other-dimensional Skartaris. Also this issue, Fury's powers, fueled by the avatar of Tisiphone, are stolen by the Cheetah. (WONDER WOMAN *vol. 2 #179*)

August: After believing that the Greek god Zeus was her male parent, Cassie Sandsmark finally meets her *real* father—Zeus in disguise! Also this issue, Barbara Minerva returns! (WONDER WOMAN *vol. 2 #183*)

September: Trapped in the past and fearing that she might irrevocably alter the timestream, Diana disguises herself as the World War II-era heroine **Miss America** and joins Wonder Woman (her own mother Hippolyta!) to battle Nazis on Dinosaur Island! (WONDER WOMAN *vol. 2 #184*)

October: The Nazi powerhouse **Armageddon** is reintroduced. (WONDER WOMAN vol. 2 #185)

Elsewhere this year, Wonder Woman clashes with Batman over a young girl accused of murder in the hardcover graphic novel WONDER WOMAN: THE HIKETEIA.

In the end, Danielle Wellys chose her own path, releasing Diana from her covenant and taking her own life rather than face capture by the Dark Knight of Gotham City.

In addition, WONDER WOMAN 80-PAGE GIANT ANNUAL #1 reprints some of the Amazing Amazon's greatest adventures from comics' Golden and Silver Ages!

In WONDER WOMAN #189, a bold new storyline began with a memory-robbed Diana being attacked by mysterious demon warriors.

2003
February: Barbara Minerva clashes with Sébastian Ballesteros for the power of The Cheetah. Minerva is apparently destroyed, while Ballesteros remains The Cheetah. Wonder Woman meets **El Cachiru**, **Salamanca**, and other South American super heroes. (WONDER WOMAN *vol. 2 #187*)

April: As the six-part THE GAME OF THE GODS begins, Diana is stripped of her costume and memory as mysterious forces seek to kill her! (WONDER WOMAN *vol. 2 #189*)

May: For the first time in her history, Diana dramatically changes her hairstyle by adopting a short style to disguise herself from unknown assailants. **Becca Doherty**, a Wonder Woman fan, is the stylist responsible for this dramatic new 'do. (WONDER WOMAN *vol. 2 #190*)

Having lost her memory, Diana searched for answers on Themyscira, where the serpentine Scylla had turned all of the Amazons to stone!

August: Donna Troy is apparently killed by a Superman-Robot. Both Titans and Young Justice mark her passing, neither team realizing that Donna may yet be alive in another dimension. (TITANS/YOUNG JUSTICE: GRADUATION DAY #3)

September: As THE GAME OF THE GODS concludes, Diana mourns the death of Trevor Barnes. (WONDER WOMAN vol. 2 #194)

2004
March: More than six decades after her creation, Diana continues to bring peace to mankind as her second series celebrates its 200th issue. Wonder Woman has never looked better or battled harder!

INDEX

ACKNOWLEDGMENTS

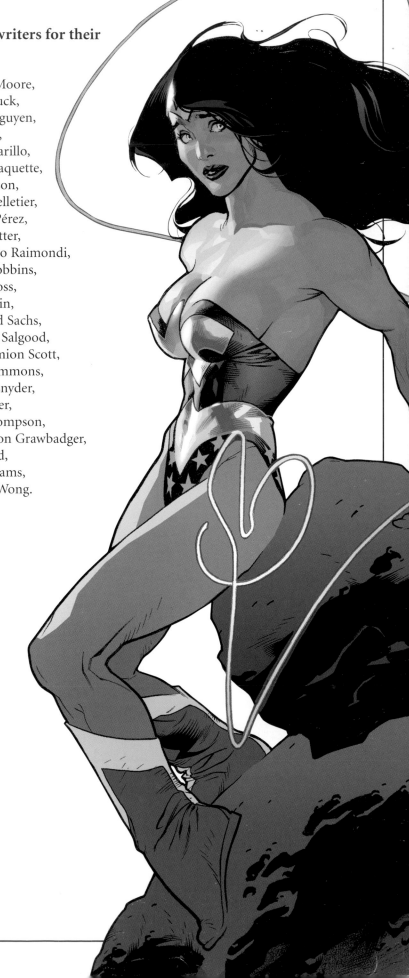

Dorling Kindersley would like to thank the following DC artists and writers for their contributions to this book:

Dusty Abell, Christian Alamy, Marlo Alquiza, Brent Anderson, Ross Andru, Shawn Atkinson, Derec Aucoin, Brandon Badeaux, Michael Bair, Eduardo Barreto, Eric Battle, Ed Benes, Will Blyberg, Jon Bogdanove, Brian Bolland, Tim Bradstreet, Rich Buckler, Rick Burchett, Jack Burnley, Sal Buscema, John Byrne, Robert Campanella, Sergio Cariello, Ernie Chan, Cliff Chiang, Matthew Clark, Vince Colletta, Ernie Colón, Jose Delbo, J. M. DeMatteis, Mike Deodato, Colleen Doran, Mike Esposito, Jay Faerber, James Fry, German Garcia, José García-López, Drew Geraci, Frank Giacoia, Patrick Gleason, Al Gordon, Mike Grell, Jackson Guice, Ed Hannigan, Glen Hanson, Irwin Hasen, Don Heck, Adam Hughes, Jamal Igle, Dennis Janke, Phil Jimenez, J. G. Jones, Robert Kanigher, Kano, Joe Kelly, Scott Kolins, Peter Krause, Andy Lanning, Bob LaRosa, Alex Lei, Eric Luke, Doug Mahnke, Mike Manley, Chris Marrinan, William Marston, Cynthia Martin, Roy Allan Martinez, Rick Mays, Ray McCarthy, Mark McKenna, Bob McLeod, Lan Medina, William Messner-Loebs, Lee Moder, Christopher Moeller,

Steve Montano, Travis Moore, Rags Morales, Todd Nauck, Allan Neuwirth, Tom Nguyen, Irv Novick, Bob Oksner, Jerry Ordway, Mark Pajarillo, Dan Panosian, Yanick Paquette, Ande Parks, Bob Patterson, Bruce Patterson, Paul Pelletier, Andrew Pepoy, George Pérez, Harry G. Peter, Greg Potter, Christopher Priest, Pablo Raimondi, Gabriel Rearte, Trina Robbins, Prentiss Rollins, Alex Ross, John Ross, Joe Rubinstein, P. Craig Russell, Bernard Sachs, Stephen Sadowski, Sam Salgood, Joanna Sandsmark, Damion Scott, Mike Sekowsky, Tom Simmons, Walter Simonson, Ray Snyder, John Stokes, Lary Stucker, Romeo Tanghal, Jill Thompson, Brian Vaughan, Wade von Grawbadger, Ron Wagner, Mark Waid, Karl Waller, David Williams, Phil Winslade, Walden Wong.

The writer would especially like to thank the following for their invaluable help in producing this book: Steve Korté, Alastair Dougall, Robert Perry, Daniel Bunyan, Ivan Cohen, Eddie Berganza, Dave Romeo Jr. and Comics on the Green, Mile High Comics, and every wonderful comic book writer and artist who has chronicled the adventures of the Amazing Amazon.

Special appreciation goes to real-life wonder woman Jennifer Myskowski, whose ability to find truth in prose requires no magic lasso.

And extra gratitude goes to Phil Jimenez, invaluable keeper of Amazon lore.

Dorling Kindersley would also like to thank the following:
Steve Korté, Eddie Berganza and Phil Jimenez at DC Comics; Hilary Bird for the index.